Theron L Hiles

The Ice Crop

How to Harvest, Store, Ship and Use Ice

Theron L Hiles

The Ice Crop
How to Harvest, Store, Ship and Use Ice

ISBN/EAN: 9783337398965

Printed in Europe, USA, Canada, Australia, Japan

Cover: Foto ©Lupo / pixelio.de

More available books at **www.hansebooks.com**

THE ICE CROP

How to Harvest, Store, Ship and Use Ice

A COMPLETE PRACTICAL TREATISE

FOR

FARMERS, DAIRYMEN, ICE DEALERS, PRODUCE SHIPPERS, MEAT
PACKERS, COLD STORERS, AND ALL INTERESTED IN ICE
HOUSES, COLD STORAGE AND THE HANDLING
OR USE OF ICE IN ANY WAY

INCLUDING

Many Recipes for Iced Dishes and Beverages

By THERON L. HILES

NEW YORK
ORANGE JUDD COMPANY
1893

PREFACE.

An attempt is made, in this volume, to record some of the more prominent features regarding Ice as it affects the health, convenience and industry of the people.

The development of the ice industry during the last forty years has been phenomenal; there are, however, but few records by which its progress can be accurately gauged.

No pretentions, other than those of a practical character, are made in behalf of this book. But it is hoped that the information here collected will meet with the favor and approval of those who are interested in this commodity.

THERON L. HILES.

CHICAGO, ILL., WINTER, 1892.

TABLE OF CONTENTS.

* The Frontispiece is from the ice harvest of the Knickerbocker Ice Co. of Chicago.

THE ICE CROP.

CHAPTER I.

AN HISTORICAL SKETCH.

The Origin of the Ice Business in the United States—Its Wonderful Development Commercially and in the Manifold Uses of Ice—A Pen Picture of a Modern Ice Harvest.

Prior to 1805, there was no regularly conducted traffic in ice, in this country. In the winter of 1805-6, a supply was secured at Boston, Mass., and the following summer a cargo was despatched to the West Indies, where yellow fever was then raging.

DOMESTIC AND EXPORT TRADE were both of very slow growth, and, in 1825, the ice consumed in the United States and exported to foreign ports was probably less than fifty thousand tons. During the thirty years following, the consumption of ice increased more rapidly, and the enterprise of the shippers carried the fame of Boston ice all around the world. Cargoes were consigned to London, to the East Indies, and the West Indies, Rio de Janerio, Calcutta, China, Japan, and Australia.

THE EXPORT TRADE reached its height about this time. Frederick Tudor, of Boston, Mass., who shipped the first cargo to the West Indies in 1806, and whose enterprise had carried

7

his ships to all the ports mentioned, was titled the "Ice King."
Not many years after this, ice and refrigerator machines
began to supply the demand for ice in tropical climes, and the
importations of the natural product soon ceased.   Two million
tons is a liberal estimate of the amount of ice stored at this
date, 1855, in the United States, with six or seven million
dollars of invested capital.

MANY NEW USES for ice have exerted a marked influence
on the demand during the succeeding years.   During the war
of the Rebellion, the Government was a large purchaser, on
account of the hospital service.   The brewers, who in earlier
days, had suspended operations during the heat of the summer, now pursued their avocation continuously, with the aid
of ice.   Meat packers found in ice an agent for immensely
augmenting their product, while the fisheries consumed many
thousand tons.

The demand for ice creams and cooled drinks, together
with the growing taste for luxuries, in our cities and towns,
has stimulated the retailing of ice until, at this time, there is
hardly a town or village, where ice privileges exist, that does
not support a representative of the ice trade, and there are few
large towns in the South which are not furnished with one or
more artificial ice factories.

THE USE OF ICE.—It is safe to say that, at this time, the
users of ice, directly or indirectly, now include nearly the
entire population of the United States.

DEVELOPMENT OF METHODS.—The progress made in the
methods and conveniences for securing the natural ice crop,
and in the construction of storage houses, has kept pace with
the growth of the demand.   Originally, axes and saws com-
prised the dealers' outfit.   Now, a modern plant is replete with
tools and appliances, whose manufacture is a distinct calling,
and may comprise vessels, cars, wagons, immense storage
houses, where upward of one hundred thousand tons of ice are
gathered under one roof, also city supply depots and wharfs,
all of which are equipped with special regard to handling
this product.

EXTENT OF THE ICE INDUSTRY.—The annual consumption of natural and manufactured ice is very great. By adding to this the equivalent, in tons of ice, of the work performed by refrigerator machines, in the various industries in which they are used, the grand total is estimated to exceed twenty million tons of ice used each year.

The capital invested in carrying on this business is not less than twenty-eight million dollars. Employment, constant and temporary, is afforded by the ice trade to about ninety thousand persons and twenty-five thousand horses.

It is probable that more than half of the world's annual ice supply is procured and consumed in this country, which is the home of this industry.

THE PRESERVING OR ANTISEPTIC POWERS OF ICE have long been made use of to keep food from decay. The best illustration of its powers in this direction is found in the accounts which travelers in Northern Europe and Asia have given us of the discoveries of huge mammoths frozen within large blocks of ice. This species of animal has been extinct for ages, and so perfectly have they been preserved that some of the native tribes occasionally make use of these supplies of flesh for food. Fish, meat and eggs are now frozen and kept during many months, and the transportation of fresh beef and mutton for thousands of miles over land and sea is an established custom. Fresh fish are frozen in the center of cakes of ice, and, shipped in this way, present a very handsome appearance.

This property of ice for domestic and commercial purposes has been of an incalculable benefit to the human family. Many eminent physicians have laid the seal of their approval upon the use of ice as a remedial agent, and also for the alleviation of suffering among the sick. So highly did they esteem it that, prior to the general introduction of the trade in ice, many doctors and managers of hospitals had private stores of ice for use among their patients. The directors of the Pennsylvania hospital at Philadelphia may be credited with being the pioneer ice dealers of that city, as in the early years of the century they disposed of their surplus stores of ice by sale in that community. Many localities which are now important centers in the ice trade were at one time dependent upon the medical fraternity for ice for hygienic purposes.

PEN PICTURE OF A MODERN ICE HARVEST. (See Frontispiece.)—Viewed from an eminence on the shore, a pretty and engaging scene is often presented at an ice house in the country, during the harvest. The clear sunlight flooding the quiet landscape discloses here and there a snug farmhouse sheltered among the hills, and surrounded with trees and shrubs, rivaling, in their soft downy draperies of spotless white and brilliant pearls, their vernal beauty when joyous spring has clothed their boughs with fragrant blossoms and emerald leaves. The broad stream or lake, ice-locked and still, stretches away to the distance, a level and unbroken plain; its farther shore dwindling away until lost to view, presents a delicately traced outline of forest and field against the horizon. The near by shore stands out clear cut and bold of outline, but quiet and deserted. Nothing in the aspect of nature denotes activity or invites the attack of man by a display of treasure.

Stepping to the brink of the hill near the shore, a new scene breaks upon the view. At the foot of the hill stands a huge ice house, its shore side serried with galleries along the entire front, with inclined ways extending from the water to the top of the house, and a connecting bridge or runway between each gallery and the incline. Alongside of the incline is discovered a power-house and tool-room, and at a little distance large barns and dwellings. From the foot of the incline leading out into the lake is seen a dark line, which branches out and becomes a large blot on the clear white surface. A closer inspection reveals an animated scene, of men armed with strange weapons attacking, with great vigor, fields of ice, which they detach from the main surface, and on which they navigate the open water, already stripped of its frozen crystals. All around are seen teams and horses drawing huge loads of snow to the distant shores, plows and markers, crossing and recrossing the cleared surface, and long lines of ice blocks, which are being floated along the channels to the incline, where the puffing engine imparts motion to swiftly gliding, endless chains, which catch up the waiting cakes and whisk them away up the incline and into the ice house, looking as though they were endowed with life-motion and were traveling of their own volition.

CHAPTER II.

LEGAL AND SANITARY MATTERS.

Ice Privileges and Legal Points—Artificial Ice Ponds and Sanitary Care of Ice Ponds and Fields.

Attention is now being given to the sanitary condition of the sources from whence supplies of natural ice are obtained. Ice sold for domestic uses and cut from canal water, must, in New York, be so labeled.

Agitation in this direction has led to the prohibition of ice cutting on specified polluted waters, by some boards of health, for any other than cooling purposes. In several States the ice crop is protected by the enactment of laws which make it a misdemeanor to destroy or injure ice in the field where it is to be cut.

No doubt the preservation of the purity of our streams and lakes will receive more care in the future, as sanitary knowledge becomes more widely diffused.

LAKES FED BY SPRINGS, and having clean beds, have naturally risen in value for ice cutting purposes. Running streams, especially those with a rapid current, purify their waters very rapidly. Exposure to light and air, the influence of oxygen, and the motion of the water, all assist in this good office. Foreign substances are expelled from the ice in the process of freezing, and streams of this character, not polluted by the presence of sewerage, waste products from factories, packing houses, gas works, etc., produce ice of great purity.

THE OWNERSHIP OF ICE FIELDS has been a bone of contention in many instances, where a knowledge of the legal rights involved would have saved expensive litigation. In a general way, ice cutting rights are divided into two classes. Ice on navigable waters is under the authority of the national government. "Navigable," in this instance, being used to denote tide water, the proprietary rights of owners of the abutting property are limited to the water line at high tides. On all such waters, navigation being closed, the ice is free and is secured by pre-emption, the first one to stake out claims being entitled to cut the ice. In contentions over boundaries of ice fields, where the issue is in doubt, the ice dealer whose property forms the water front is given the preference.

Rivers, small lakes and navigable streams above tide water are termed public. The boundary line of abutting property is held to extend under the water to the center of the channel, and includes the ownership of the ice formed above it. Public convenience for navigation and commerce, however, take precedence. The rights to this ice are thus subject to contract and sale. The submerged land may also be sold, and all deeds to water front property should clearly set forth the boundary line and all the rights that are guarded and reserved.

WHERE DAMS ARE BUILT across streams and the water line is raised on property beyond the limits of that held by the owner of the dam, consent must be obtained from the holders of property thus affected.

There are numerous creeks and brooks which are fed by springs, or have their source in spring lakes, which make excellent ice fields, with very little labor or expense. Advantage may be taken of low lands in the vicinity of such streams. Gravel forms the best bed for ice ponds, as it is free from weeds. In some of our lakes, occurring in districts abounding in gravel, the water is pure and sweet and the gravelly bed can be seen at great depths. Springs are usually numerous in such localities.

The following methods of preparing dams can be employed in some situations. The depth of the pond and the force of the current of the stream are to be taken into account in fixing upon the proportions and construction of dams. Also the quantity of water usually running into the pond and the largest amount likely to be received during a season of flood. If the soil is a light loam, or a seam of gravel is near the surface, dig a trench down to a hard bottom, and on the pond side drive in a row of stout boards, breaking joints and sloping them toward the dam. Behind this paling fill in with clay rammed down. A crib formed of logs notched and bolted together, and lined or faced with plank on pond side, should be set at the rear of the sub-paling. This crib is filled with stones and clay or sand. The front is banked up with earth and covered with rip-rap.

The center of the dam is provided with a sluiceway large enough to carry off flood waters, and, at the bottom, a pipe or a box well bedded in cement gives a current on the bottom which carries off sediment. It is also useful in taking off air and gases, which, arising from the bottom, form air bubbles in the ice. Some water should always pass over the upper sluiceway.

Dams may be formed entirely of an embankment of earth and stone. Their base should not be less than their height, with increased thickness where pressure from a current has to be resisted. Shallow dams may be formed by driving two rows of plank across the line of the dam, and filling in the inclosed space with rammed clay. Break joints in the planking, and bolt stringers along the top edges to bind them firmly together.

IN CHANGING THE COURSE OF STREAMS, cut the new channel deeper than the old one, to insure the current following it. Straightening or changing the course of a stream will often improve the topography of a farm and drain wet or marsh land.

Food fish, which can readily be raised in these ponds, forms a welcome addition to the family larder.

THE PURITY OF BROOKS which feed ice and fish ponds should be preserved. No filth should be dumped into them or on their banks. Stables and cesspools should not be situated where they will drain into them. Vegetable refuse and litter, which may be brought down with the current, should be caught by screens and removed from time to time, or they will accumulate in the pond and injure it.

CHAPTER III.

CUTTING AND STORING ICE.

The Science of Ice Formation—Preparing the Ice Field for the Harvest—Getting Rid of Snow—Sudden Thaws and How to Remedy Their Damage—Tools and Implements Used—Thickness of Ice—Care of Ice Tools—Filling the Ice House —Closing it up and Caring for It—Shipping Ice from the Field.

With the advent of a sharp freeze, attention is directed to the ice field, from which a harvest is hoped for at no distant day. The purification of the water has been given attention before this time, together with all preliminaries relating to the plant in its various and complex features. The weather now determines the lot of the ice dealer. As the cold breezes whistle over the water, stirring it into ripples, and breaking its surface into waves, a wonderful change is rapidly transforming its liquid pearls into flinty diamonds. Gradually the heat in the water is radiated into the air. As fast as the surface water is cooled, it is condensed, and sinks to the bottom, its place being taken by the warmer and lighter water from beneath. Gradually the entire mass reaches the point of maximum density, at $39\frac{1}{4}°$ F. Below this temperature, until it reaches 31° F., water expands as it is cooled. Now the surface water no longer sinks as it grows colder, being rendered lighter by expansion than the water beneath. Upon reaching 32°, convection, or freezing, takes place, and the surface assumes the solid form.

CARE OF THE ICE FIELD.—From this time until the crop is stored in the ice house, the ice dealer devotes his energies to the care of the ice field. Special situations develop special duties and requirements, which the alert dealer studies with care. If the ice is on a running stream, the possible pollution of its higher levels will be carefully guarded against, and also all rubbish removed from the surface of the field. Sticks and stones bedded in the ice hinder the work and damage the keen edges of the cutting tools. Motion in the water is necessary to promote the growth of the ice, and, when the ice is sufficiently heavy, traveling over the surface, or other jarring, is beneficial. It has been found that where a roadway has been opened across an ice field, and the travel over it considerable, the ice was thicker along the roadway than at other places on the field.

On inclosed lakes or mill ponds, a gentle current induced in the water promotes the growth of the ice materially. The air is expelled from the water during freezing, if opportunity is found for it to do so. Unless this is done, the ice is cloudy. Agitation of the water assists the escape of the air ; hence it is that ice from running streams is usually clearer and more brilliant than pond or lake ice. An outlet afforded to the land-locked ponds and lakes is often beneficial during ice-making weather. Too rapid a current, however, will retard growth, and a gentle motion diffused over the entire field produces the best results.

The growth should be carefully noted under different conditions, attention being given to the atmospheric influences and other general effects, and the regulation of the motion, based on ascertained results at the locality where applied. As the ice thickens, its growth is slower at the same, or even a lower, temperature than that which at first made ice very rapidly. The earth at the bottom and sides of the ice field radiate heat into the water. The heat rays of the sun pass through the ice, if it is clear, into the water below, with very little effect upon the ice itself. The ice, being a poor conductor of heat, is, under these conditions, an obstacle to its own growth. It shuts in the water from contact with the cooler air, prevents agitation of its surface by passing breezes, and retards the escape of air and heat.

On running streams, these conditions are much modified. In passing over shallows or rapids, where the current is swift, the water remains open and exposed to the air. At these points in its course it parts with its accumulated air and heat very rapidly, a thin vapor or mist being often perceptible in the air at such places, owing to the rapid radiation. The tumbling and turning of the water at rapid shoals materially assists the growth of ice at points below where the current grows gentle. Streams of this character, whose beds are free from accumulations of vegetable mold, or other sources which generate gases, produce clear and sparkling ice of greater thickness than is found on still ponds or lakes in the same vicinity, and exposed to the same temperature.

THE USEFULNESS OF SNOW.—Snow, as it is well known, is a great impediment to the inroads of frost into anything enveloped by it. A covering of snow on an ice field is a great impediment to the escape of heat from the water, as well as protecting the ice from the direct action of the cold air, and greatly retards the growth of the ice. It is essential to remove this snow as early as practicable, as the ice harvester has always in view a possible thaw or rain, and endeavors to secure his crop at the earliest practicable moment.

Snow, however, in the event of soft or warm weather, is an aid to the ice by protecting it from the direct heat of the sun, and the force of a rain is largely expended in melting the snow. The water and snow on the top of the ice freezes into snow ice as soon as the weather turns cold again. This snow ice is white, being very porous and filled with air, and detracts from the quality of the crop, its thickness depending on the depth of snow on the field, amount of water, and the temperature. At the top of this snow ice, where it merges into the snow, will be found a stiff, crusty layer, more or less firmly united to the ice below, which adds to the difficulty of removing the snow on top. An inch or two of snow ice will lessen the loss by breakage of cakes, in stowing, and the ice also comes out of the house in better shape, and will stand shipping better. It is not so brittle as clear ice, and is homogeneous in its structure, not being readily split in any direction.

REMOVAL OF SNOW.—Various methods and appliances are in use for the expeditious and economical removal of snow. As soon as the field will bear the weight of a horse, scrapers of various designs are placed at work. If the ice is too thin to support a horse safely, flooding is resorted to. At intervals of six feet, more or less, according to the freedom with which

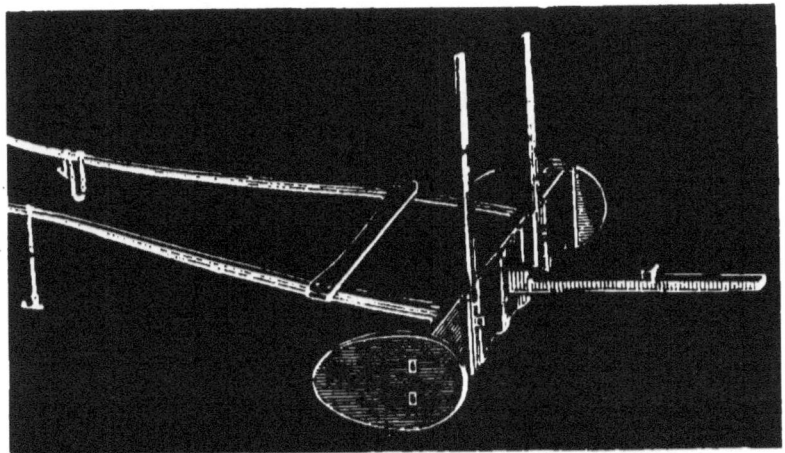

FIG. 1. CLEARING OFF SCRAPER.

the water rises through the openings, holes are cut through the ice, and the water saturates the lower part of the snow.

This helps to thicken the ice rapidly, and, if the weather is cold, it will very soon be heavy enough to support a horse. As soon as this is the case, the scrapers are placed at work. The snow ice thus formed is afterward gotten rid of by planing, if more than an inch or two in thickness. If the snow is light, and not too deep, it is scraped into windrows, by scrapers similar to those in Figs. 2, 3 and 4.

2

FIG 2.

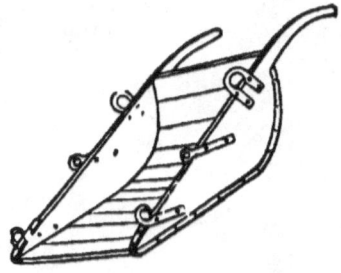

FIG. 3.

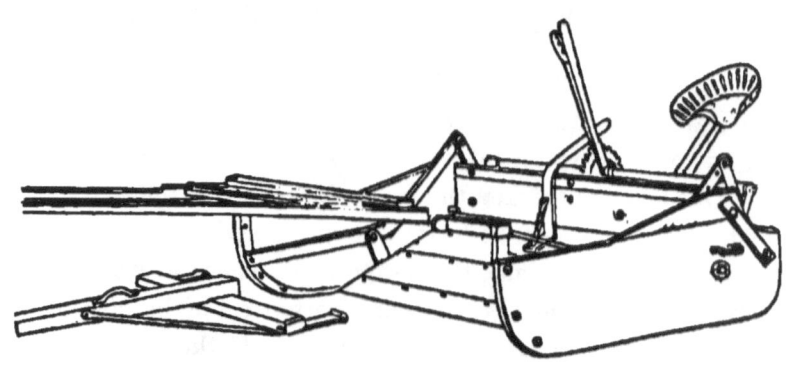

FIG. 4.
SNOW SCOOP SCRAPERS.

These windrows are distributed over the field, not being made large enough to sink the ice at any point. Scoop scrapers are now employed, which gather up the windrows and carry the snow off to the shore, or to a distance from where the ice is to be cut. If the field is very large, and the snow deep, dumping points are selected on the field. The weight of the snow will sink the ice at these points, and cracks will soon loosen the dump from the main body of ice. A deep groove plowed alongside of the dump will assist in loosening the dump, and keeps the water off the field. Some of these scoop scrapers are constructed with great care, and nicely adapted to the needs of the ice harvester.

A SUDDEN THAW during the winter, while the ice crop is forming, is an annoyance to the ice dealer, and, if accompanied by rain, the field will often suffer by being flooded with water from the surrounding hills. Sand and earth may be washed on to the ice, making it dirty and injuring its quality. Water standing on top of the field will soon comb and rot the ice. If only an inch or two of water is on the field and the weather turns cold, it can be left to freeze and then be planed off.

If it is deep it can be readily handled, by cutting holes through the ice, or tapping the ice field in a number of places; the water, being heavier than the ice, will sink and raise the ice, if it has opportunity of so doing. Tapping should have prompt attention, and the water removed without delay. Even if the water freezes on top, the ice is not of good quality and is not part of the ice below. It forms a layer which is attached to the old ice, but yet is not solidly a part of it, and gives trouble by splitting out in barring off. Ice expels the air while freezing principally toward the bottom, and as it has no chance for escape through the ice beneath, the top layer will show a white streak.

For tapping the field the auger and the tapping axe are used. If the water is accumulating rapidly and despatch is wanted, the axe will be found the more rapid-working tool.

The auger, however, makes neater work, and leaves the field
in better shape—often an important desideratum.

THE OUTFIT FOR HARVESTING.—Time is of great value in
handling ice in any of the various operations gone through
with on the field or in the house. Delays during harvesting
greatly increase the cost of getting ice prepared for the market. Great care and much study have been devoted to per-
fecting the paraphernalia by which the ice crop is handled, as
will appear as the reader follows the round of duties of the ice
harvester. In some emergencies the crop is only saved from
partial or complete loss by the despatch which modern devel-

FIG. 5.   ICE AUGER.

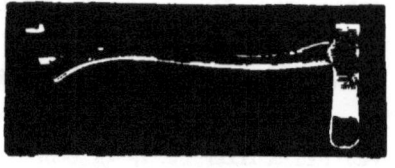

FIG. 6.   MEASURE.   FIG. 7.   TAPPING AXE.

opment of tools and machinery has placed at the command of
the enterprising ice dealer. The advent of warm weather during the harvest demands the utmost celerity in all departments, if the crop is secured.

More credit than is generally supposed to be warranted is
due to the splendid energy and managerial ability of the ice
harvester, during seasons when the home ice crop is a partial
or entire failure. No one, not practically familiar with the
business, can readily understand the extra strain and burden
imposed on the ice dealer who succeeds in securing supplies
sufficient to meet the requirements of his customers, by going
to the far north for this most beneficent and useful product of
nature. Enterprise pays in this, as in any business.

Having removed the snow the field is carefully inspected,

and quality and thickness of the ice ascertained in all parts. The field is bored with the ice auger, and the measure indicates the thickness. The auger is withdrawn and the appearance of the ice noted before the auger reaches the bottom and water fills the hole. If the snow ice is too heavy it must be removed.

Two methods for doing this are available. It can be cut loose and broken into chips with the snow ice planer on the

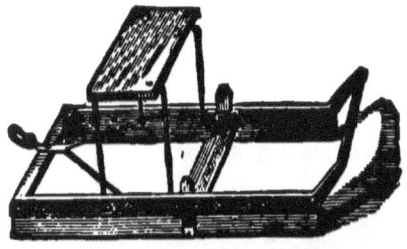

field, the chips being afterwards cleared with scrapers and scoops; or it can be left on the ice and cut away by the elevator ice planer as the ice cakes pass up the endless chain ice elevator incline, on their way into the ice house.

FIG. 8. FIELD PLANER.

The first method is in use wherever the endless chain ice elevator is not employed. When it is to be removed by the field planer, the ice field is first laid out and plowed to the depth of the snow or sap ice to be removed. The snow ice planer follows the plowed grooves, cutting off the refuse ice.

THICKNESS OF ICE.—Generally speaking, the ice is desired at an average thickness of fourteen inches; this being convenient for subsequent handling. In practice, the thickness of the ice, as it is stored or shipped from the water, varies with the exigencies of the season and the average thickness formed at the locality.

In the latitude of Central and Southern Ohio six-inch ice is often stored; in the vicinity of Chicago and Omaha, ten inch; in Maine, sixteen inch, and in Minnesota, twenty inch. Ice, thirty inches thick, has been cut and stored on Lake Superior, in Northern Wisconsin, where ice forms equal in purity and brilliancy to any found in this country. The ordinary printing on the pages of a Chicago newspaper has been easily read through a block of Lake Superior ice twenty-nine inches thick. At Winnipeg, Manitoba, ice is cut forty inches in thickness. Such thick ice keeps the year through.

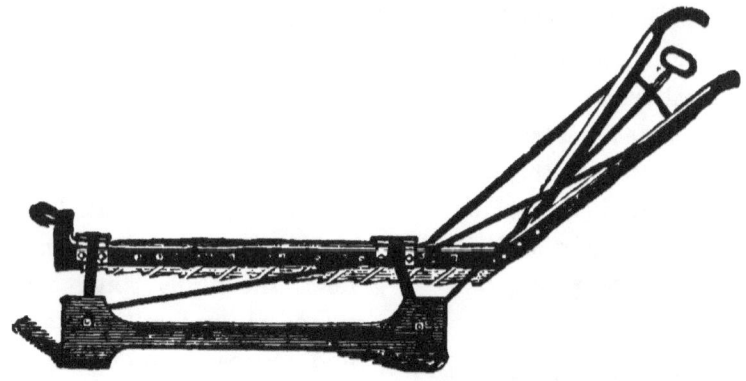

FIG. 9.   MARKER, WITH SWING GUIDE.

FIG. 10.   FIELD PLOW.

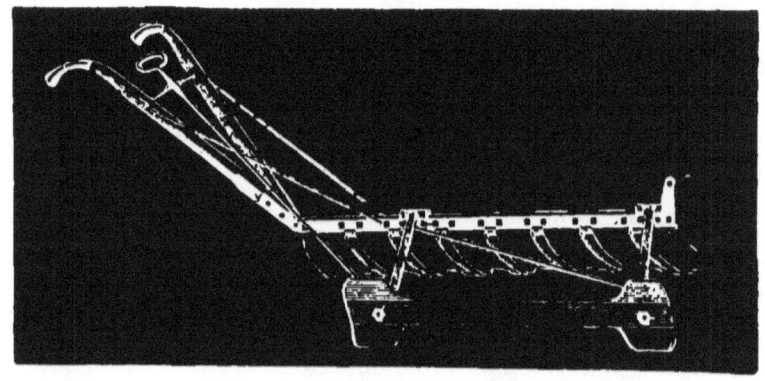

FIG. 11.   SWING GUIDE PLOWS.

LAYING OUT THE ICE FIELD.—As the ice field is inspected and mapped out for plowing, all unsound places, air holes, or shallow places where rocks or sand bars approach near to the surface, are marked for avoidance. A convenient method is to bore holes at such places, and plant pieces of brush in them. Thin ice, formed where the ice has been removed during cutting, is also marked in this manner, to give warning of the danger of venturing upon it.

Like a good general, the ice harvester takes note of the physical advantages of his position. If he can so lay out the field that the current and prevailing winds are in his favor and assist to float the ice toward the house, his strategy is not without reward. Room for refuse ice is needed where it will not impede the ice floating toward the house. The lay of the shore line must not be overlooked, on streams where the current is strong, in calculating for support for the shore ice. The best ice in the field will always be secured as a prime consideration.

Quality should always be of the first importance, and, in these days of close competition, pure ice is necessary for success in the ice business. Ice, for any purpose, should never be cut from impure or contaminated water. Too much care can not be given to securing clean, pure, healthful ice for all uses, directly or remotely allied to preserving or curing food products. Natural ice from pure crystal water is one of nature's purest productions.

Having gone over the field and determined the plan of operation, the first task is to lay out the base lines from which the marking and plowing are gauged. Stakes are planted at either end of the line, and a heavy cord drawn taut between them. The hand plow is now passed alongside the line, making a score in the ice from end to end. Sometimes a long board with sights is used for laying out the first line, and a line marker is a cheap substitute for the hand plow. The teeth of the horse marker are now set in the hand plow groove; the guide is unlatched and runs along on top of the ice. Care

FIG. 12.   HAND PLOW.

FIG. 13.   PLOW ROPE.

FIG. 14.   LINE MARKER.

is taken to keep the marker upright, by firmly supporting the handles. This cuts a groove three inches deep. The blade of the guide is now placed in this groove, and the marker cuts a new groove parallel with the first one.

This operation is continued until the field is grooved in parallel lines over its surface in one direction. Plows are now started in the marker grooves, and are run back and forth until the grooves have been cut about two-thirds through the ice, care being taken to leave not less than four inches of solid ice below the bottom of the groove.

Meanwhile the marker is at work scoring the field in lines at right angles to those first laid out. A large wooden square with legs about fifteen feet long is used to square from, and the field is marked and plowed in both directions.

When the snow ice plane is to be used, the field is marked out in one direction only. The depth cut is regulated by a planer gauge, attached to the marker, to the thickness of the snow ice to be removed. The runners of the plane set in the grooves and are guided by them.

CHANNELS AND CANALS.—The marking and plowing being well under way, the channels and canals require attention. Where the current is gentle, and on ponds and lakes, the opening of the channel and canals is not attended with much difficulty. Where the current is swift, as on the large rivers, practical skill is required in opening up the field. The pressure of the current makes it difficult to open the channel and canals, and the shore ice is in danger of giving way. Stays and braces are sometimes employed to anchor the shore ice, and to prevent the channels from closing.

In some instances it has been found advisable to have the channel permanently fixed by piles driven into the bottom of the river on either side. In others, braces are set in the ice, at short intervals, before the channel is opened, as shown in the illustration. The posts should be heavy, and the cross struts may be ten or twelve inches square. The post holes, if cut oblong, will allow short boards to be spiked to the sides of the posts at their lower ends. When inserted through the ice, a quarter turn of the post will bring the projecting ears under the ice, and no trouble will be given by the post raising out of its place. The cross strut should just allow the ice to float beneath, and be well secured to the posts, which require inclined braces, joining the posts opposite the ends of the struts, with their feet planted in recesses cut into the ice. Water should be poured around the braces, and when the braces and posts are frozen in place a very strong support is secured against the current, as the following cut shows.

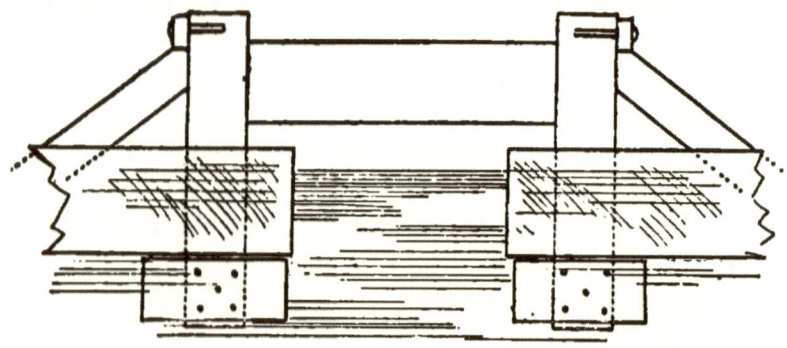

FIG. 15. BRACES FOR CHANNEL WITH SWIFT CURRENT.

Where the current is not so strong, square frames may be employed. They are placed in the channel where the ice cake will float through freely ; their sides should fill mortices in the sides of the channel, and not project into the path of the cakes, as shown in Fig. 16.

Various methods of dealing with cracks in the ice have been tried. A good one is to take long planks and extend them across the cracks laying flat on the surface. By boring through the planks into the ice, and inserting wooden pins, the loosened portion is firmly held, and the cracks will freeze up. If the pins are inclined in opposite directions a firm hold is secured on the ice.

When the channel has been located, if convenient, a deep groove is plowed at either side, and the remaining ice is cut away with the pond ice saws. Splitting chisels are now brought into play, and the ice in the channel is split up into cakes, which are sunk and floated under the ice. Canals through the plowed field are similarly opened. The field is now in readiness to furnish a supply of ice cakes for stowing in the house.

A section is selected, and the grooves carefully double calked with chips, from the plowing, to prevent the water running in. For this purpose a calking bar is used. Ice saws are now brought into requisition, and the grooves at the ends of the section are sawed through to the back. The groove at the back is now struck into at several points with one or another

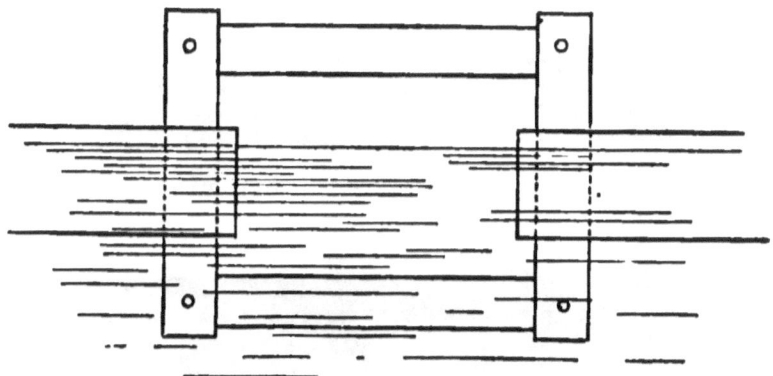

FIG. 16. BRACE FOR SLOW CURRENT.

of the barring off tools provided for this work. A section called a float, and containing one hundred to one thousand or more cakes, is readily split off. The tools used for this work vary with the thickness of the ice and the size of the floats. The fork bars are the most often used, the two-prong bar being the favorite on heavy ice. If the first cuts with the saws are so made that the ice cut away is a little wider on the bottom than on the top, and the sides parallel, it will facilitate getting out the first float cut away. By sinking the float a little all pinching or binding at the sides is prevented.

The floats are split into rows of single or double cakes, as they are floated near to the channel leading to the incline. As

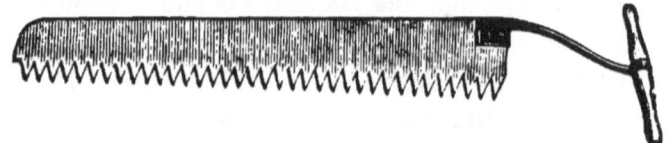

FIG. 17.   BEST CAST STEEL ICE SAWS.

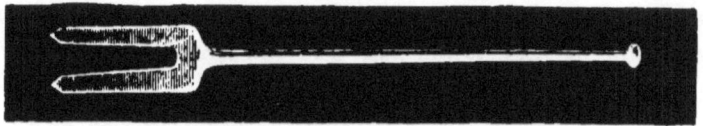

FIG. 18.   TWO-PRONG FORK BAR.

FIG. 19.   THREE-PRONG FORK BAR.

FIG. 20.   FOUR-PRONG FORK BAR.

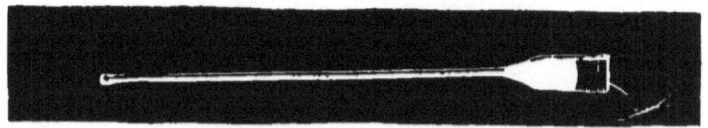

FIG. 21.   CALKING BAR

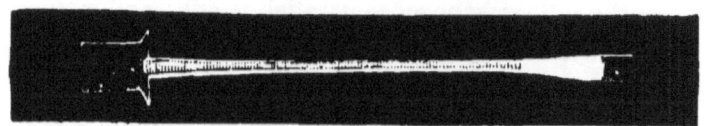

FIG. 22.   BREAKING BAR.

the long rows are moved into the channel, a man, standing on a bridge a few inches above the ice, strikes a needle or splitting chisel into the plowed grooves as they are passed beneath his feet. One or two dexterous thrusts will cleave the ice to the bottom. In frosty weather, with the ice hard, it can be split true and square, in most instances. Cakes not smoothly split must be trimmed before they reach the incline, and the bunches removed.

The work on the field is directed to secure a supply of ice cakes at the foot of the incline, in advance of the requirements of those whose duty is found in placing the cakes in position within the ice house. No more than will be run into the house, and also leave the channel full, with some floats near at hand at quitting time, should be detached from the field.

Ice floats left too long before being broken up into single cakes, are in danger of having the grooves flooded, and wholly or partially frozen up. In this condition they are either worthless or split up with much labor and great irregularity. The single cakes left in the channel over night serve to prevent it being closed with ice in the morning, and the delay incident to opening it up is avoided.

Some early work, however, is always needed on the channels. The single cakes will have a connecting web of new ice, which must be broken up and trimmed from the sides of the channel and the cakes. The broken ice and damaged cakes which are not wanted must be kept clear of the channel at all times. The larger pieces may be sunk under the ice, and the smaller ones be removed by the scoop nets or sieve shovels. A snowstorm during the harvest is attended with much discomfort to the ice harvesters. The channels are filled with slush, which packs around the floats and cakes, making their progress slow and laborious. It eludes the scoop net and is very hard to deal with. The field is soon buried out of sight, and must be cleared and scraped with as little delay as practicable.

HOUSING THE ICE.—There is room for large latitude for variations in the methods employed on the ice field. The situations are so different that the dealer is called upon to exercise judgment and ingenuity, in determining what is best to be done. On swift running streams the ice, after first forming, may be broker. by storms, and with a return of settled weather, will freeze in rough and confused masses of broken ice in places. At other points no floating ice has found lodgment, and the second freezing is regular and of good quality. In order to secure the ice from these favored spots, the harvester may be obliged to open a channel several miles in length, and float the ice down to where his storage houses are located.

At the foot of the incline at which the ice cakes are taken from the water, and along the channel directly leading to it, the ice is subject to much wear. The work necessarily done on the cakes as they are floated through this channel, requires the presence of a number of trimmers and bar men at this point, as well as those who are feeding the cakes into the elevator, or placing them in position for the grapple. The tools used at the foot of the incline and near by channel are illustrated on Pages 00-00.

There is often an accumulation of refuse ice taken from the channel and thrown on the ice not far away. Ice cakes sometimes slip from the grapples on their way up the incline, and slide down, striking with great force at the foot of the incline. All these, and other sources of wear, on the ice, make it important to provide some protection to the sides of the channel, and, as the edges soon dip below the surface of the water, a footing or walk for the channel men. Where elevating by means of grapples, it will be found a convenience, and often the means of avoiding delays, to have a water box or trough sunk in the channel, at a depth to admit the cakes passing freely on to the lower end, and yet near enough the surface to prevent the cakes ducking, or dodging under, when pressed forward from the rear. The jackman, as the slack is taken out of the line and the pull is felt, bears a firm grip on the handle of his grapple, and, at the same time, bears down heavily, and ducks the heel of the cake, engaged by the grapple,

FIG. 23. ICE HOOKS.

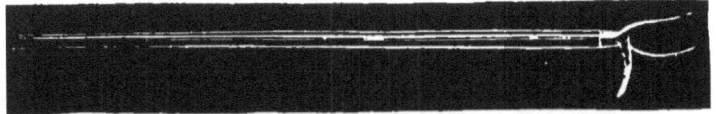

FIG. 24. ELEVATOR FEEDING FORK.

FIG. 25. CHAIN SCOOP NET.

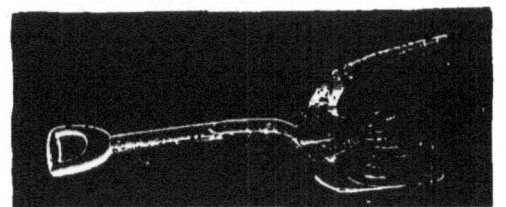

FIG. 26. SIEVE SHOVEL.

FIG. 27. RING HANDLE SPLITTING CHISEL.

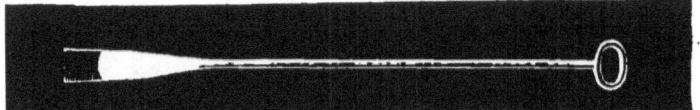

FIG. 28. CHANNEL HOOK CHISEL.

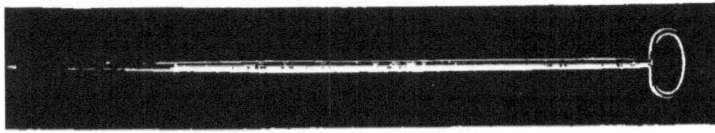

FIG. 29. NEEDLE BAR.

under the water. The men who are placing the cakes for the
jacks, if the ice is heavy, bear down on the cake with their
pike poles at the same time, to prevent the last cake from
being ended over. The water box is necessary, at these times,
to steady the cake below, and prevent it sinking too deep.
Several cakes are usually run up at one trip. A sharp lookout
is necessary on the part of the jackman, and some experience
is required to become an adept at handling the grapple. Seri-
ous accidents have resulted from careless or ignorant methods,
and caution should be observed by all who are employed about
the field, incline, or ice house. The construction of the water
box varies with the depth of water and amount of ice run
over it. Usually it is of a temporary character, and renewed
each year. Order and a thorough system should be carefully adapted to the work on the field and in the house, by
every ice harvester. Details, fully worked out, and the plan
once in force, it should be strictly observed by the proprietor,
and exact compliance insisted upon from all employes. Unless
discipline is maintained, especially on large fields, much loss
of time and money will result, and life and limb be jeopardized.

CARE OF ICE TOOLS.—Provision for preserving the cutting
qualities of tools is of great importance. An inferior tool, or
one out of repair, will detract from the efficiency of the labor
employed to use it. The amount depends on the particular
kind of work under consideration, and the comparative condition of the tool with which it is done. Attention to this matter
is often neglected, from a failure to properly estimate its
importance, or from a mistaken idea of the ease with which
an incompetent or ignorant man can spoil the best implement
which can be made. Ice saws, of the best type, will, when
new, cut rapidly and true; one or two dressings, done in the
wrong way, will detract from their cutting efficiency one-fourth
or more, and it will be impossible to cut true with them.

One man should be trained to correctly dress the saws, and
then be held responsible for their work. When the teeth are
worn short, or the saws are sprung, send them to the ice tool

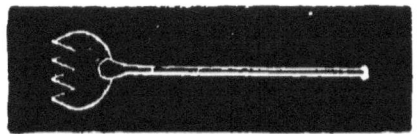

FIG. 30. TOOTHED TRIMMER BARS, IRON HANDLE.

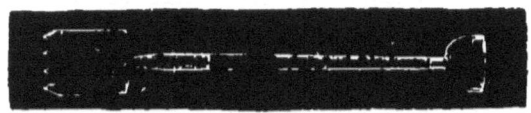

FIG. 31. TOOTHED TRIMMER BARS, *D* HANDLE.

FIG. 32. JACK GRAPPLE.

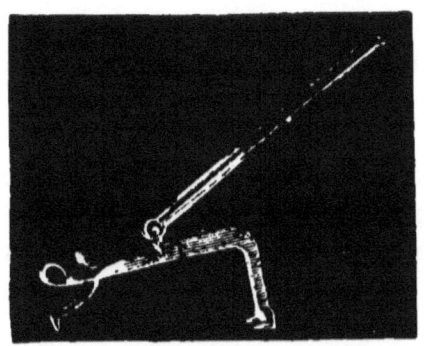

FIG. 33. HANDLE GRAPPLE.

FIG. 34. CHANNEL GRAPPLE.

manufacturer, to have the teeth gummed out to their correct size and shape, and the blades straightened and stiffened. Ice plows are frequently rendered useless by improper dressing or careless handling. The range and proportion of the teeth, as they are when new, must be kept up, and the cutting points sharp and keen. The heels and bottoms must be dressed down regularly with the points,—no more, no less. Only a man of known ability should be allowed, under any pretext, to dress the ice plows.

Any delay in plowing may involve the loss of part of the crop, and any detention of the work of those detaching the cakes from the field, from a lack of plowed surface to work upon, may prove to be the cause of an hour or more time lost or frittered away by nine-tenths of the entire force employed, both on the field and in the house. Nine-tenths of the entire wages, for an hour or more, is thus lost to the owner, and an incompetent workman is the apparent cause. The lack of management and system is, more likely, the source of this waste.

Plows which have been worn so they cut hard, need gumming out, or reforging, or both. Plows and markers are the chief cutting implements of the ice harvester. Too much care cannot be taken to make a proper selection, originally. The best plows are now made with steel beams and steel bolts. They are superior to the old style iron plows. The guides used on plows and markers should have no lost motion, at any point, when the guide handle is latched in place. The latest improvements are in the trussed form of guide, which is perfectly rigid, and the double hinge and swivel method of securing the handle to the guide, combined with the pin and mortice latch. This construction produces a plow and guide which has no looseness in any joint, and is so braced that the plow cannot depart from a vertical position unless the guide is raised out of its groove.

All ice cutters who have had their fields marked in curved, instead of straight, lines, with the resulting wrenching or breaking of plow teeth, will appreciate and welcome this improvement. Bars, tongs, and hooks should be kept sharp, and, when out of repair, sent to the maker, to be brought back to a condition of efficiency. The close of the cutting season is the best time to select and ship to the ice-tool maker all implements which require overhauling.

A tool room should be provided, of sufficient size to store all cutting tools, scoops, scrapers, and extras of all kinds that are liable to breakage or rapid wear. Space should be reserved for a filing bench, having a large north light, and a grindstone —driven by power when practicable—for sharpening bars, hooks, and tongs. Where the ice houses are large, and in isolated positions, the tool house, if well fitted up, is of great assistance, affording the means for making repairs of an urgent character. A good set of millwright tools, together with a well-chosen supply of seasoned timber, of such sizes as are used in the various runs and connections, will often repay their cost in a single season. Large boarding houses are often found included' in the ice harvester's inventory. This is a necessity where the storage houses are situated any distance from towns or cities. Several hundred men are sometimes thus accommodated.

FILLING THE HOUSE.—Ice should be housed during freezing weather, if possible, as the cakes will then enter the ice house dry and hard. In soft weather the ice is soft, and contains some water; the cakes, being chilled in the house, are frozen together, causing an increase of labor and breakage in getting the ice out for shipment during the summer. When the ice is heavy, of best quality, and stowed, during freezing weather, in a well-constructed ice house, it can be kept for two or three seasons, and then be taken out in good condition, with but little extra loss by breakage. It should have attention at all times, however, and be kept in perfect order.

The various methods which are in use for elevating the ice cake from the water into the ice house, or on to the platform, will be noticed in detail, under a special chapter devoted to this important branch of the mechanics of the natural ice trade.

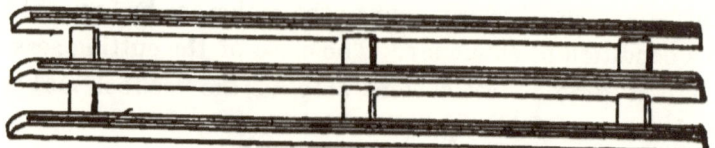

FIG. 35. WOODEN SKID. NO. 1.

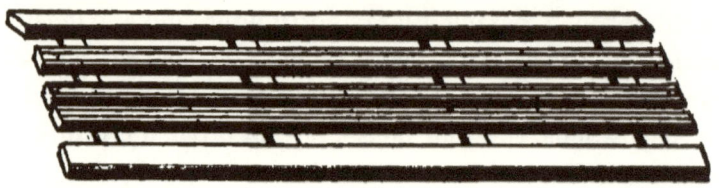

FIG. 36. WOODEN SKID. NO. 2.

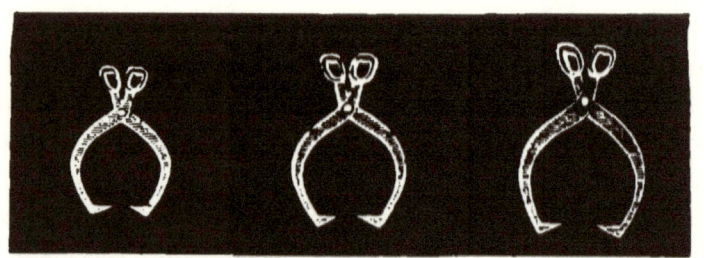

FIG. 37. WAGON AND LOADING TONGS.

FIG. 38. PACKING CHISEL.

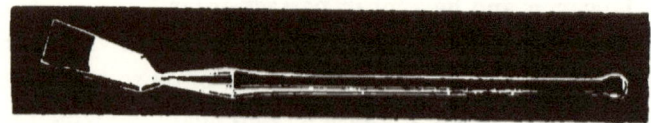

FIG. 39. PACKING CHISEL.

The ice cake, as it enters the ice house, does so on a skid, or run, which is placed at an inclination, the end nearest the entrance higher than the end leading in toward the center of the room. At its lower end the skid is connected with another having the same general inclination, and thus a continuous line of runs is formed, extending from the entrance to the farther part of the room. The inclination of these runs is determined by the distance the ice is to travel on them, and the height of the galleries on the front of the ice house.

The runs are usually arranged with a rapid descent near the entrance, and the further end, on a level with the intermediate portion, graduated between these extremes. When the inclination imparts too high a speed to the cakes, a break is set into the runs. It usually consists of a board, in which a number of large nails are driven, with their heads left projecting above the surface. This board is set in the line of the runs, or attached to one of them, so the under surface of the ice scratches on the nail heads. The number of nails and the depth of the scratches is easily varied to suit the velocity required.

As the ice cakes are run into the ice house, they are stored at the farther end first, and are gradually filled in toward the front. Through the back and center of the room, stowing is most rapidly performed. Filling the front end, and under the runs, require more time and care. The ice cakes are moved into place with ice hooks and tongs. As the cakes pass along the runs, they are caught with the ice hook and guided off the run, at either side, as desired. The runs are made flat, with no projecting sides or rails. Two lines of the V-shaped run iron are placed on the runs, and the ice will follow them, but is readily slipped off when wanted. The accompanying cuts show the common patterns of runs, and the tools used in the house during packing. .

The hooks, tongs, and runs are used in directing the cakes to their final positions. The bars, chisels, and adze are used to trim any inequalities off from the cakes, and, in some cases, to level off each layer of ice as it is stored. This is not so often done, when ice is stored for shipment from the house, as in cooling rooms, when it is desired to pack as much ice as possible.

PACKING ICE IN THE HOUSE.—The method employed in arranging the ice cakes varies in different parts of the country, The important thing to keep in mind is the amount of good, merchantable ice possible to be gotten out of the house, as it is shipped away during the warm season. This does not depend upon how much can be crowded in, but upon the packing and

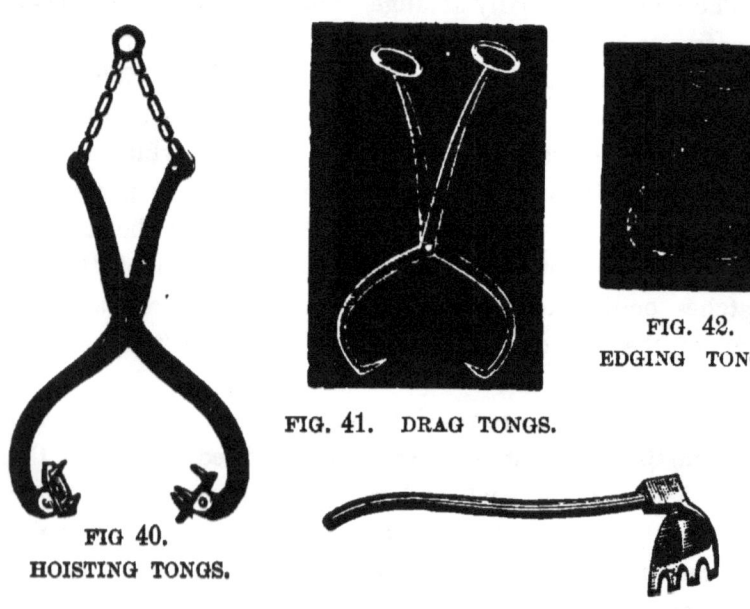

FIG. 41. DRAG TONGS.

FIG. 42.
EDGING TONGS.

FIG 40.
HOISTING TONGS.

FIG. 43. ICE ADZE.

arranging of the cakes. Two things are to be observed in this, prevention of waste by melting, and ease in loosening or detaching the cakes, as they are taken out. The following method may be taken as an example, and varied as good cause is found for so doing.

If the ice is thin, place the two first courses on edge. and pack as closely together as practicable. The succeeding courses place in flat, or in the same position they occupy on the water. Arrange the cakes one directly above the other, and leave a space of two inches on all four sides or edges. In every five or six courses, joints are broken. The last four or five courses on top are placed, each one, to break joints, and closely placed at edges. The reasons for this arrangement are, that the ice on the floor of the house wastes rapidly, and, by placing the cakes on edge, the minimum loss is obtained, and the succeeding cakes, placed one above the other, and free on the edges, having only the top and bottom surfaces in contact, the minimum breakage and labor, in loosening cakes, is obtained; also, by breaking the joints every few courses, the circulation of air currents, which is very destructive to the ice, is shut off, and, finally, the top courses close in the mass thoroughly, and prevent the top covering from sifting down into the body of the ice.

The chapters on loss of ice by wastage in the house, and the construction of ice houses, will present more fully some of the considerations bearing upon the methods of stowing the ice.

In some localities the ice cakes are all placed upon edge. Among the advantages claimed for this method are, ease in loosening and taking out the cakes, and the closer packing secures more ice, where storage room is limited. There is a risk of damage to the ice house, by the pressure of the ice against the side walls, when packed in this manner. The edges, being uneven, tend to throw the ice out of plumb, or to give the whole mass an inclination in one direction. In stowing, care is required to keep the spaces between the cakes free from chips or broken ice.

No more trimming than is necessary should be done in the house, and the crowding of cakes together on the runs, and in sliding them to their places, should be avoided. Broken cakes should not be allowed to come into the house, and, if cakes are broken in placing, they should be thrown out of the house.

Experience and practice, in the handling of runs and managing the progress of the stowing of the ice cakes, attest the value of system in this department. To do the necessary work with as much despatch as possible requires close attention to details, and watchfulness, that the labor and efforts of the men are properly directed and distributed.

The runs outside the house are permanent, and arranged in ghlleries, about five feet apart, with connecting runs from each gallery to the incline. The top run is placed well up to the plate. At each intersection of the incline and runs to the galleries, there is a gate, which may be removed from the face of the incline, thus affording access from the incline to the runs. The gate at the lower run being open, the ice cakes all pass on to the first run, and enter the house at this height. When the house has been filled with ice to the height of the first run, or one or two courses higher, the level of the house is then too high to handle the ice over the lower run. The incline gate is now placed in position, shutting off the first run, and the ice is raised upon the incline to the height of the second run, and passes into the house at this level.

It is now necessary to rearrange the runs within the ice house. They must be uncoupled from the first gallery, and raised up and secured at the height of the second gallery. The under blocking and bracing is removed, and the runs set to one side. Before they are disturbed, a number of ice cakes are run in, and left near the entrance, to be stowed in the space the runs and staging occupied, directly in front of the entrance. Unless care is taken, this filling in will be done with irregularity, and more or less broken ice will be left among the good cakes, causing loss by wastage and breakage, when the house is opened up. This filling in under the runs suspends the ordinary work of stowing, and is attended with some loss of time.

After the cakes are all in place, the house runs are raised up, blocked and braced in position, the connecting runs coupled on, and a new line of runs conducts the ice from the second gallery to the further part of the room.

A system of winding drums, placed in the roof timbers, with ropes attached to the runs, at either end, saves time and labor, in adjusting the house runs to the levels of the different galleries; also, in shifting them, as they are raised to the level of the courses, as the cakes are placed.

CLOSING AND CARING FOR THE HOUSE.—When the room has been filled to the level of the wall plate, the ice is covered with dry planing-mill shavings or sawdust, ten or twelve inches deep. The entrance opening is closed, and filled in with sawdust, or other packing.

The harvest being secured, the ice house carefully closed, and all chance for circulation prevented by a top dressing, it requires regular attendance once a day, to trim the top covering, if any part of it should sink into the crevices between the ice cakes.

As the warmer days and spring rains set in, the proper ventilation of the ice house is important. All steam or vapor arising from the ice should be gotton rid of as soon as possible. The various plans which are in use to attain this end, will be found in the chapter on wastage and care of ice in the house.

As soon as the tools for harvesting are no longer required for use, they should be promptly gathered together, and inspected. All that have been broken, or damaged, should be bundled up and consigned to the manufacturer, to be put in thorough cutting order, and returned to the ice house, in the early fall. All other tools should be carefully cleaned, and all bright or polished steel coated with oil, to preserve from rust, cases strapped to plows and saws, and all neatly packed away in tool house, which should be dry. Snow scoops and scrapers are better for an occasional coat of paint, and, if stored in a dry, cool place, sheltered from the weather, will last much longer. It is a good plan to have all the tools inventoried directly after the cutting season, and they should be marked with the owner's name or initials.

The elevator machinery should also be inspected, and any defects noted, for early repair, the apron raised from the water, and the water shaft and fittings cleaned, and thoroughly oiled. The ice chain, if given a coat of slushing oil, will take no harm. All machinery which is exposed to the

weather should be thoroughly coated with slushing oil. The
engine should have attention, and all working parts be preserved from rust. All the brass trimmings on engines or boiler
should be taken down, boxed, and stored in a secure place.

SHIPPING ICE FROM THE FIELD.—While the ice house is
being filled, winter shipments of ice may be made to points
where supply stations are maintained distant from any cutting
privilege. Large shipments are often made to points south of
the frost line, or where the crop is deficient. To accommodate
this traffic, loading platforms are built with connecting runs
from the lower incline run. A switch is arranged by which
the ice cakes can be directed, either on to the loading platform
or into the ice house. Long trains of cars can be filled daily.
At a single platform, ten to fifteen cars are loaded at one time,
while a double platform will accomodate double the number.

If the side tracks are placed at both sides of the platform,
no time will be lost while cars are being switched, a train
loaded on one track being switched out, and the track filled
with empty cars, while loading proceeds in the cars on the
other track. Diagrams of these platforms are shown at Fig.
52. Endless chains, with bars at short spaces, pass along the
top of the platform, and carry a cake, at a regular speed,
before each bar. (See Fig. 51.) A short doorway slide is
placed between the car and platform, and a man, stationed at
the car door with an ice hook, slides the cakes into the car as
fast as the stowers can place them.

CHAPTER IV

CONSTRUCTION OF COMMERCIAL ICE HOUSES.

The Earliest Forms of Ice Storage—Development of the Modern Ice House—The Site and Its Requirements—Placing the House—Survey—Foundations—Size of an Ice House—Details of Construction for a House Embodying all Modern Improvements.

The earliest reference to the use of snow for cooling purposes occurs in Holy Writ, and carries us back about three thousand years. History records the custom which prevailed among the Romans, of storing snow upon the mountains during the winter, which was made use of in the summer for cooling beverages. Vaults, or pits, of circular form at the top, and tapering to a point at the bottom, were scooped out in the ground. The sides were lined, and the top thickly thatched with straw, after being filled with snow, which was tightly packed. The doorway was through the top. A modernized Roman snow cellar is shown in Figs. 44 and 45, which is taken from a cellar in use in Virginia. Its successor in the transition to more modern designs is seen in Figs. 46 and 47.

Before ice was cut and stored for commercial uses in this country it was secured, in many instances, by those who used it in their business. Brewers, dairymen, butchers, and some physicians, had ice vaults, or cellars, constructed on the Roman method. The first commercial ice houses were built below the surface of the ground. Gradually they emerged into the light and air, being only partly below the surface. Brick, stone and wood were in use for building materials. Gradually, experience leading the way, the ice dealer has evolved the modern ice house.

THE MODERN ICE HOUSE represents many years of development, and has a scientific, as well as a practical, value.
Improvements may be expected in this as in other branches of
the ice business. The discoveries and inquiries which scientific and practical men are continually making in this direction

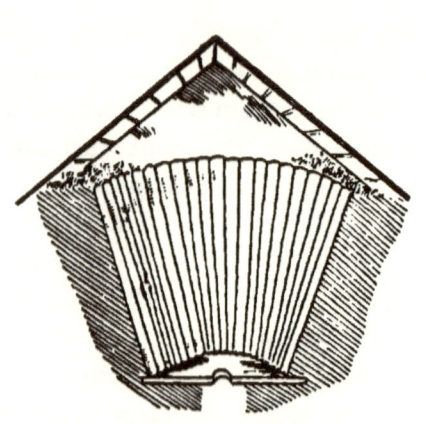

FIG. 44.   INTERIOR VIEW OF OLD
STYLE ICE CELLAR.

FIG. 46.   MODERN ICE PIT.

FIG. 45.   ROOF OF SAME.

FIG. 47.   ITS CONSTRUCTION.

are rapidly adding to our store of knowledge. Ice houses, as
now built and furnished, give few suggestions of their original
prototype.

THE SITE.—Many features are combined in a really good
site for a commercial or large ice house. Good ice in ample
quantity, a porous soil, easy accessibility both from the water
and land, proximity to market; also cheap and efficient trans-

portation. Observance of the first and last of these points is imperative. Where natural drainage is lacking, the deficiency can be supplied, and access effected, in most instances, if the other features warrant the expense.

In selecting a site, when the lay of the land will permit, place the length of the house north and south, and arrange the incline and runs with as few turns as practicable. The ice cakes require assistance to keep them in motion on a crooked runway, and are constantly being jammed and spalled. On a direct run of proper pitch the cakes will travel without attention in freezing weather. On warm, sloppy days, when the ice is soft, it will require assistance. The platforms for winter shipments *via* rail come in for attention in placing the incline, which should be conveniently disposed for supplying them with ice cakes as fast as they can be handled. System and dispatch are the watchwords of the ice dealer while ice cutting is on.

SURVEY AND FOUNDATION.—The location and size of the house being determined, a survey is made and all lines staked out. It is important to have the foundations square and of the exact size, so that dimension lumber and roof trusses will fit as designed. Levels, also, call for attention, and the entire site should be brought to grade.

In the construction of foundations practice varies. They are partly dependent upon local conditions and climatic influences. For large houses, where the wastage is readily drained off and the sills are comparatively dry, they are about as durable as the balance of the building when placed directly on the ground.

The life of an ice house varies from so many causes, that no limit can be given applicable to all cases. When the lumber is well selected and the construction thorough, fifteen years of constant service will tell plainly on the building. If repairs are made as often as required, its term of usefulness is extended.

In warm climates, also for smaller houses, and for city supply depots, foundations of stone or brick are employed to

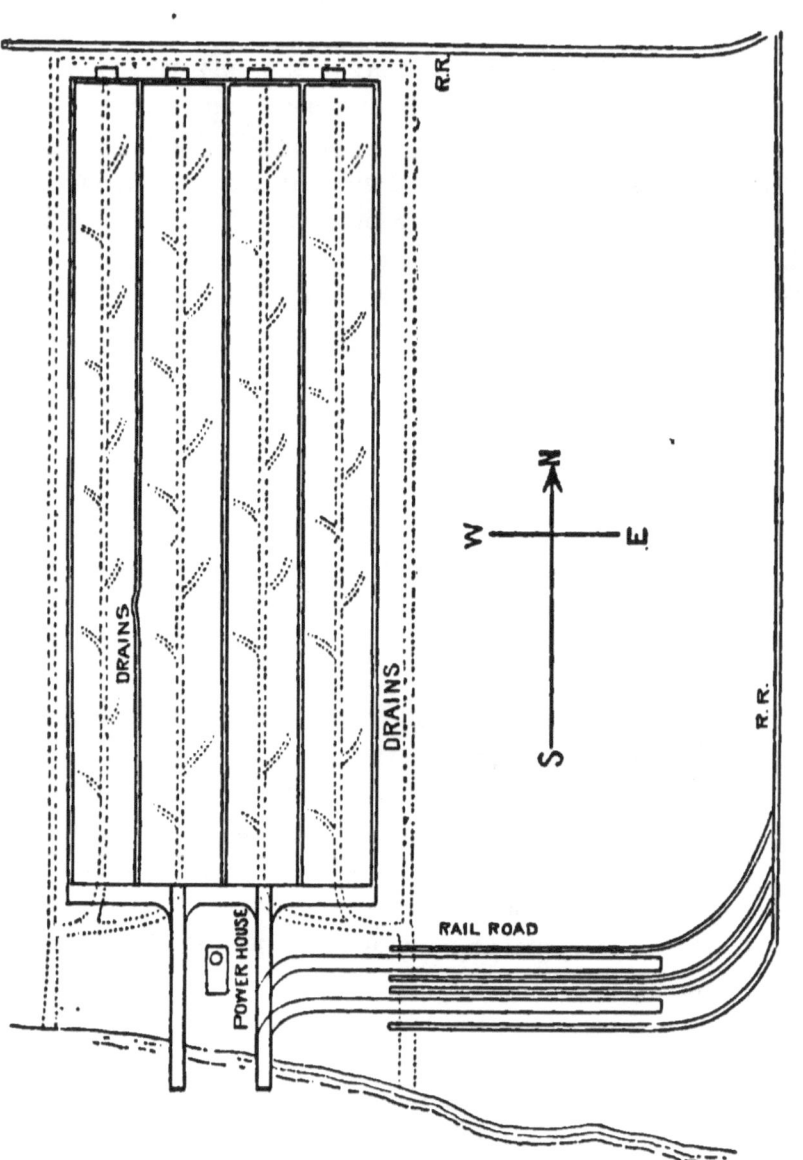

FIG. 48. PLATE A. GROUND PLAN.

advantage. They should be put in below frost, and extend about two feet above the surface.

DETAILS OF CONSTRUCTION.—In the building illustrated in plates *A*, *B*, the sills are placed upon the ground. The house is divided into four rooms, each forty feet wide in the clear, two hundred and fifty feet deep, and forty feet high from sill to plate. The dimensions of lumber required may be:

For outside sills, 8 x 10 inches, of such lengths as can most readily be obtained.

Inside sills, 6 x 10.

Outside posts 4 x 10 inches x 40 feet, set 12 feet apart.

Studding, 3 x 10 inches x 40 feet, with three feet centers.

Inside posts, 4 x 8 inches x 40 feet. Studding, 3 x 8 inches x 40 feet.

For outer circulating air space, the studding should be 2 x 8 inches x 40 feet, with three feet centers.

For inner dead air spaces, 2 x 6 inches x 40 feet studding are placed upright 12 feet apart, and horizontal cross studs 2 x 6 inches x 12 feet and three feet apart, are filled in between. This makes spaces 3 x 12 feet on the inside of all the outer walls.

Plates on the outer walls are 3 x 10, and on inner walls 3 x 8 inches.

The main studding is lined on both sides with moisture-proof sheathing, and boarded up with matched lumber. The inclosed space is filled with non-conducting substance, usually sawdust or spent tan bark. The filling must be dry and packed tightly.

The inner 2 x 6 studding is lined with sheathing, and then boarded up with matched lumber. The joints of this studding should be made with care and the lumber selected, no crooked stock being used. Sealing up these joints with pitch adds to their efficiency, and also to the durability of the lumber.

The outer studding is covered with weather boarding or ship siding. Twelve inches at the bottom are left open and hinged covers swung over them, which can be opened or closed as ventilation requires.

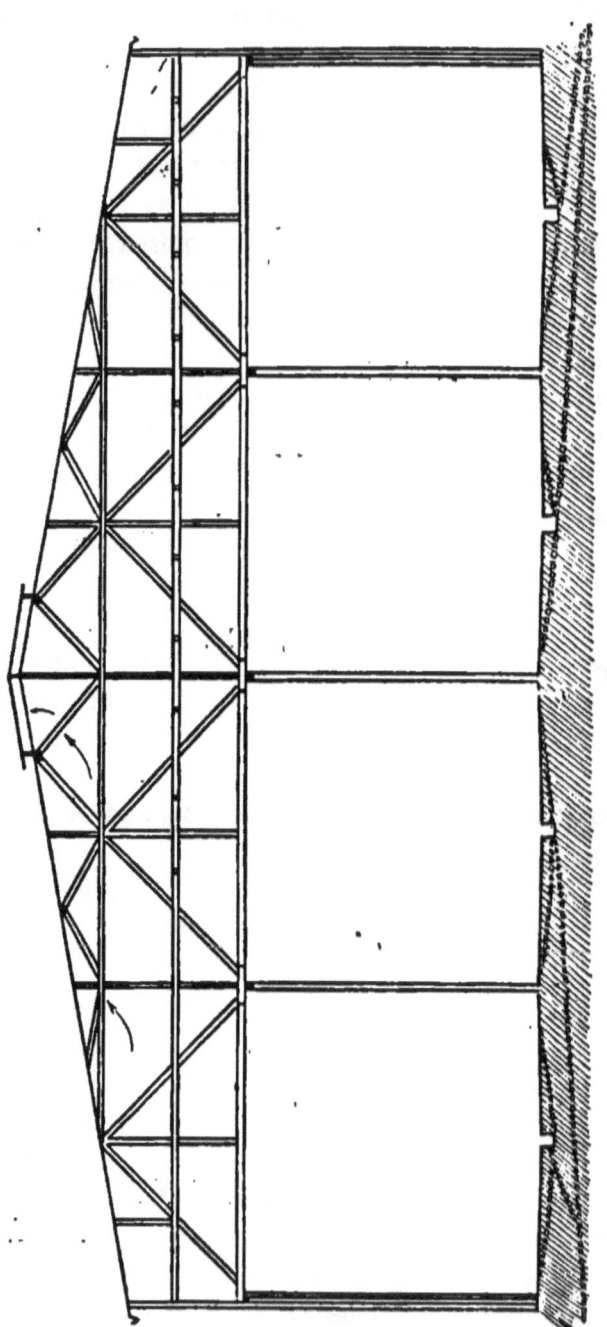

FIG. 49. PLATE *B.* CROSS SECTION.

The interior walls have 4 x 8 inch x 40 feet posts, and 3 x 8 studding, which are boarded on either side with matched lumber and filled.

The lower section of these walls, to a height of ten to fifteen feet, is often left without filling, as it is more exposed to the ill effects of moisture, and requires renewal before the upper portion. This is more conveniently done where no filling is in the wall.

In the center of each room, on the end at which the ice cakes enter, an opening is left extending from the sills to the plate. As the house is filled with ice these openings are closed up. Boards are provided, when building, which will fit into place and make the walls at these openings, as near as practicable, the same as in other places. The middle section being filled and planked by the inner and outer air spaces.

At the opposite end of the rooms a similar opening is provided. For closing it a slightly different plan is adopted. The outer section is divided into doors five or six feet high, swung on hinges; these take the place of the weather boarding. The interior wall is then arranged the same as the one at the opposite end of the room. These doors can be opened as the ice is coming out, and remain closed at other times.

Interior partition walls are sometimes of value. It is thought they add to the durability of the house, and also effect a saving in wastage. In the majority of houses they are dispensed with.

The construction of the roof will be found convenient and substantial, if the plans shown in Plate B are followed. Light-colored roofing composition should be used, avoiding tar and gravel, or tin, as these both attract and absorb the heat. Gable roofs, with good shingles laid four or five inches to the weather, are the best roofs for ice houses. They are cooler and more durable than most composition coverings.

The posts in Diagram B can be extended and additional bracing put in. The increased area and weight will require a proportional addition to the strength of roof timbers. In the

4

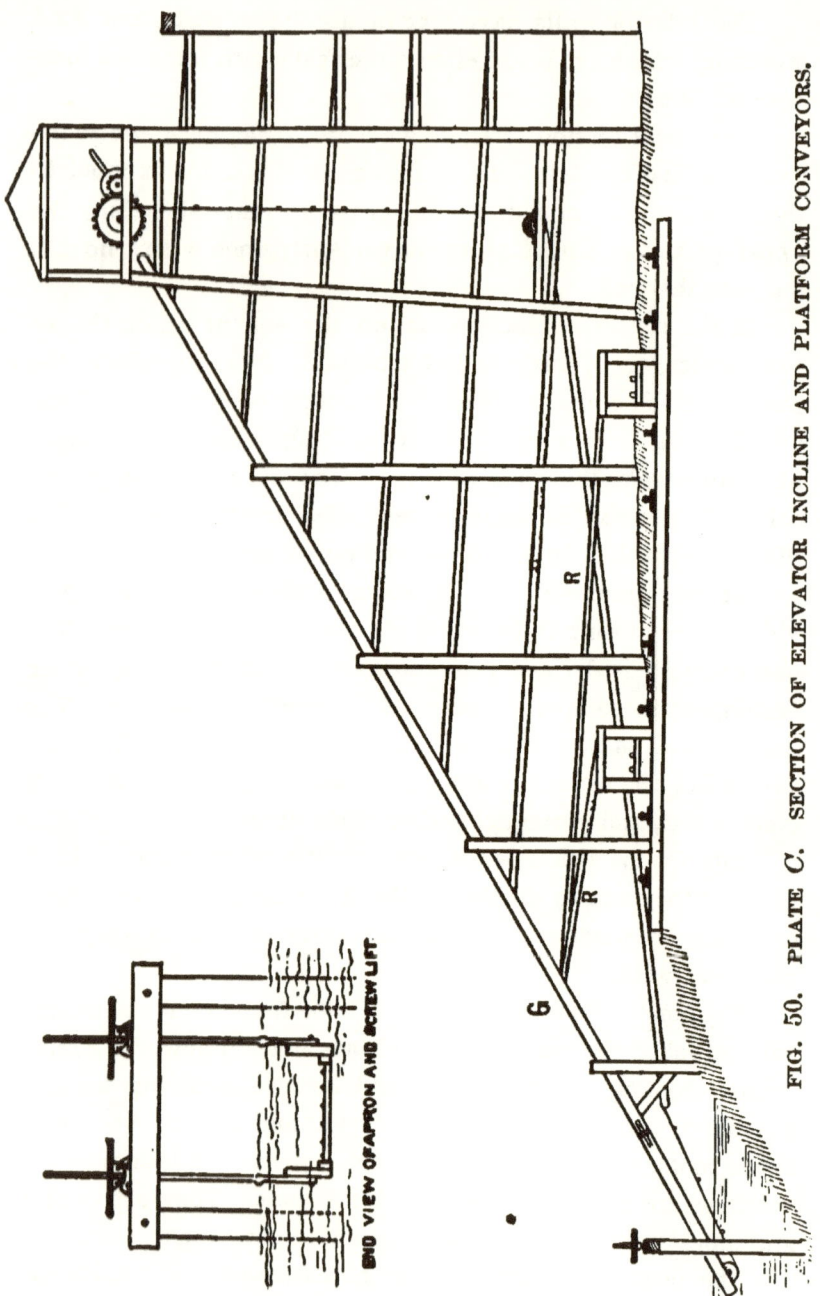

END VIEW OF APRON AND SCREW LIFT.

FIG. 50.   PLATE C.   SECTION OF ELEVATOR INCLINE AND PLATFORM CONVEYORS.

sizes of timbers for ice house construction, noted in this chapter, consideration has been given to durability, and while lighter material is employed, in some instances, the houses are sooner racked and sprung out of place.

The ventilator on top is about twenty feet square and two feet high, with slats on all sides. It will not be required on high gable roofs, an opening in each gable end being sufficient to carry off the moisture and heated air. The gable ends should be well braced against the wind.

At the center of roof trusses a floor is laid through the building, dividing the space above the ice. Trap doors are cut through this floor about seventy-five feet apart, four to six feet in size; these doors are for ventilating the space between the ice and the floor, and for dumping the sawdust through on top of the ice. It also affords a convenient place in which the sawdust can be stored and dried, when the houses are cleaned in the fall.

The outer circulating air-spaces are continued to the level of the loft floor, discharging the air into the loft, where it finds vent through the ventilator.

The eaves project about two feet, and are provided with ample gutters, which are furnished with large conductor pipes every fifty feet. On the side of the house where galleries are placed, the roof is extended to cover them, or, if at a gable end, a special roof is provided.

Lightning rods are especially required on ice houses. Being often the most prominent object in their locality, the electric fluid finds its readiest path through them, and the escaping vapor and much of the material used in their construction add to their exposure. Copper strips, terminating in forked points, raised above the cone of the roof, fifty or seventy-five feet apart each way, provide ample protection. A line of points across the house should be connected, and the copper strips extended, without any break or interruption, into the ground. They should be buried several feet below the surface, and if they terminate in a drain or other damp place, their efficiency is increased.

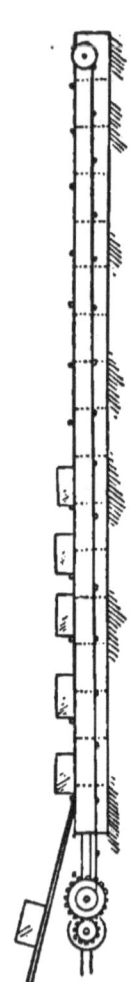

FIG. 51. ELEVATION OF PLATFORM ALONG TRACKS FOR LOADING CARS.

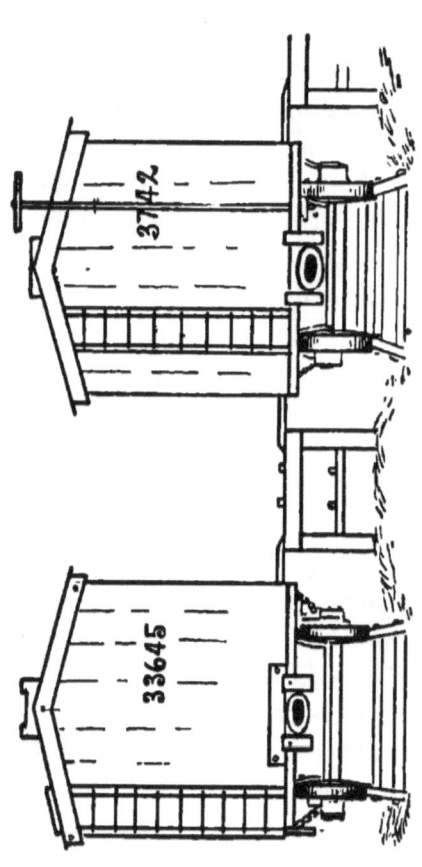

FIG. 52. PLATE *D*. SECTION OF LOADING PLATFORMS.

The floor of each room is graded slightly toward the center, and a trench dug through the center from end to end. It should have a grade toward the front of the house of about two inches in a rod. At the rear of the house it may be nine inches square, gradually increasing to double this size at the front of the house. Lateral drains, alternating on either side, are desirable. If the surface drainage sets toward the house, it should be intercepted and condcuted away. After the trenches are made they are filled with broken stone or cobbles about nine inches deep at the start, and double the depth at the front of the house. The side trenches may be six or eight inches wide, and filled about the same depth.

On top of the stones, shavings, straw, reeds, or other porous filling, is placed, to the level of the floor. The entire floor is now covered with a layer of charcoal, or with coal ashes placed several inches deep. On top are laid boards, not too closely placed, with length toward the main drain. The spaces between the boards form channels to conduct the waste water to the drains. Where the drains emerge from the house they are trapped, to prevent any air currents from entering through them, and collected into one or more main channels.

Plate *A* illustrates the drainage plan, and a section view is presented in Plate *B*. In porous soils, which can be depended on to carry off the wastage, drains are not so necessary. For very large houses, however, they should not be entirely neglected. In warm climates and for city supply houses, cement floors are the best.

For loading cars for winter shipments, the platforms illustrated in plates *A*, *C* and *D* are used for handling large quantities. The ice cakes are elevated on the incline to runways (see *R*, in Plates *A*, *C* and *D*), and slide by gravity until landing on the platform. An endless chain with cross-bars passes over the top of this platform, carrying a cake before each bar. Where a railroad siding is placed on both sides of the platform the work is expedited, as no delay is occasioned by waiting

for cars, a loaded train being pulled out and empty cars run
in on one track, while loading continues on the other.

THE INCLINED WAYS shown in Plate *C* are rigged with
endless chains, which carry cross-bars. In filling the house,
the ice cakes are floated to the foot of the incline, and fed on

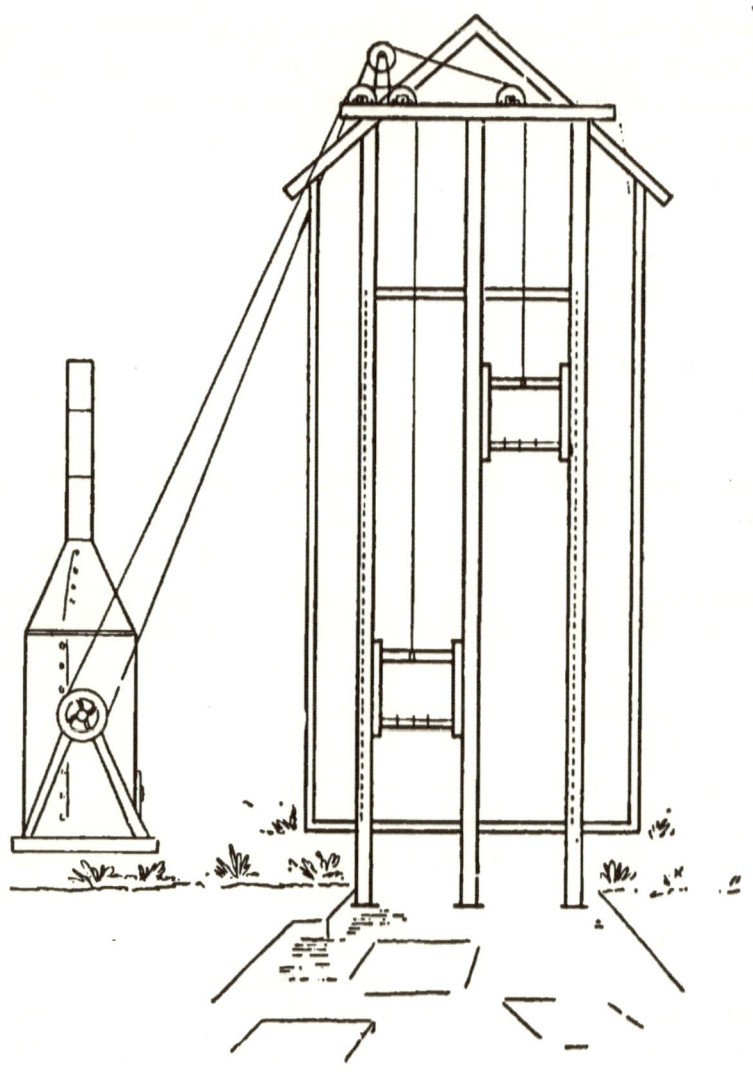

FIG. 53.   PLATE *E.*   HOISTING GIGS AND REVERSING ENGINE.

to it, one or two cakes at a time in front of each bar, and thus is made to travel up the incline. The cakes are passed through gates on to the runways at the various levels desired, and pass over these, by gravity, into the ice house.

There are two methods of arranging the chains—called the over-shot and the under-shot. The first named is mostly used, and is the one shown in Plate C. The power required varies with the length of the incline and with the style of the elevators, which are arranged for one or two cakes on a bar. The smaller rigs are operated with an eight or ten horse power engine, and the larger plants up to one hundred horse power, where several elevators and platform conveyors are coupled on to one engine. For filling smaller houses there are several methods in use, a choice depending on the surroundings and size of the room or house.

Next in importance to the endless chain system, are the jack grapples by which large quantities of ice are annually stored. An incline is used which is similar to the one shown on Plate C, but of lighter build. These grapples are operated with horses, or with steam power, when winding drums are employed. By using friction-winding drums, the jack grapples readily accomplish the work of a single elevator, and are less expensive. This plan is shown in Plate E. An ordinary threshing engine furnishes ample power, and this method is rapidly growing in favor. Where the ice house is placed at the edge of the water and there is no room in which to place an incline, the gigs are very convenient. When they are operated by means of a winding drum run by a reversing engine, and large enough to handle four cakes at a time, they are very efficient. Economy of power, simplicity and ease of management, are all in their favor.

Small houses and cooling rooms are filled with the aid of hoisting tongs.

CHAPTER V.

CARE, HANDLING AND MARKETING OF ICE.

Care of Ice in the House—Leaking and Waste, How Prevented
—Getting out Ice—Lowering Machines—Ice Shipments—
Marketing Ice—Ice Wagons and Outfits.

After a house is filled with ice and put in order, it is placed
in the care of an attendant. The top dressing requires frequent inspection to keep it intact. Keep the circulating air-
chambers in the walls in operation, except when the air is
humid; at such times the lower openings are closed. The loft
is ventilated directly into the cupola on top of the roof, which
also carries off the warm air currents rising through walls.

THE WASTING OF ICE.—Ice in the house is attacked by
water, moisture, vapor, warm air and evaporation. Pressure
of the mass upon the lower courses assists in their destruction,
and heat from the earth is also radiated into them. Evaporation goes on, to some extent, at all temperatures; its immediate effect is cooling, as it carries off heat. Water rots and
wastes ice more rapidly than warm air. Water permeates the
mass and destroys the ice, while warm air affects only the
exposed surface. Vapor is wasteful when it settles down on
the ice and is condensed. Air currents, if they are strong, cut
away the ice very rapidly, and will sometimes comb the ice.

Keeping the room as air-tight as possible tends to preserve
the ice. Whenever the house is opened the warm air enters,
and vapor will collect above the ice. This should be given an
opportunity to escape, by opening the ventilator doors in the
loft floor.

As the ice is taken from the house, the covering of sawdust should be kept in place over the ice as far as possible. If

56

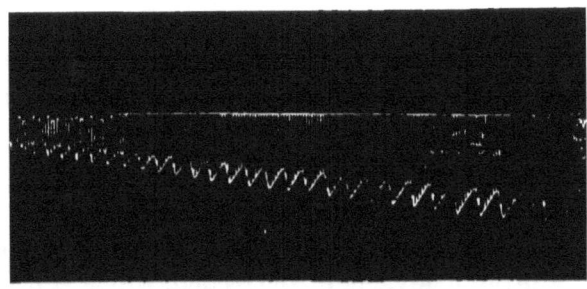

FIG. 54. HOUSE ICE SAW.

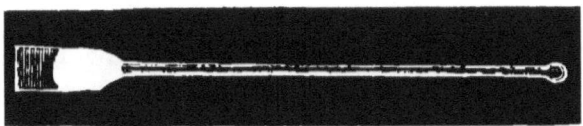

FIG. 55. RAISING CHISEL BAR.

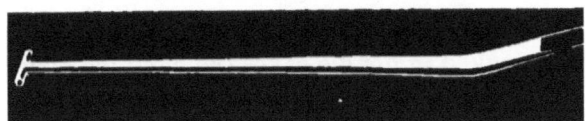

FIG. 56. STRIKING-UNDER BAR.

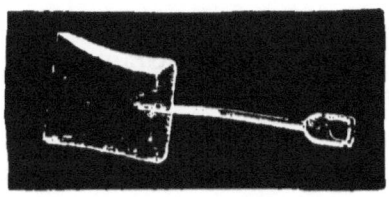

FIG. 57. DUNNAGE SHOVEL.

the space over the ice is sealed up, the air, being above the freezing point, becomes saturated with moisture, which settles upon the ice, softening and melting it. When the outside air is cooler than that over the ice or in the loft, the moist air is driven out, if the ventilators are open. Hence, in clear weather, the ventilators should be opened at night. In foggy or damp weather, ventilators should be kept closed.

IN TAKING OUT ICE from the house, it is a good plan to take out three tiers across the house at once. The upper tier is worked a little in advance of the second, which is in advance of the lower, or third, course. This gives a sloping front, on which ice from the top can be lowered without breaking, and work can progress on the three courses at the same time. The covering can also be readily handled.

The tools employed are the house ice saw, raising-chisel bar and striking-under bar. The saw has a narrow point, with a double row of teeth for cutting down into the crevices around the cakes, and a handle arranged to place pressure on the point of the saw. The raising-chisel-bar is used for cutting around the sides. The striking-under bar is struck under the bottom of the cake, to loosen it from the cake beneath. Where ice has been packed in double cakes the hand ice plow is sometimes employed to open the grooves, and the splitting chisel for separating the cakes. The ice is run out to the door on the house runs, or skids. The house tools not illustrated elsewhere are shown below.

LOWERING THE ICE.—There are several methods employed for dropping the ice down from the top of the ice to the level of the cars or wagons below. Gravity is the force usually employed. Ice-gigs, with a counter-weight to return the empty gig to the level of the ice, are, in one form or another, mostly in use. They can be mounted on a wheeled platform, and moved from door to door, as desired.

PACKING FOR SHIPMENT.—When ice is loaded into cars it is covered with marsh hay; any crevices at doors or windows are carefully packed with hay, to keep out the air. Shavings

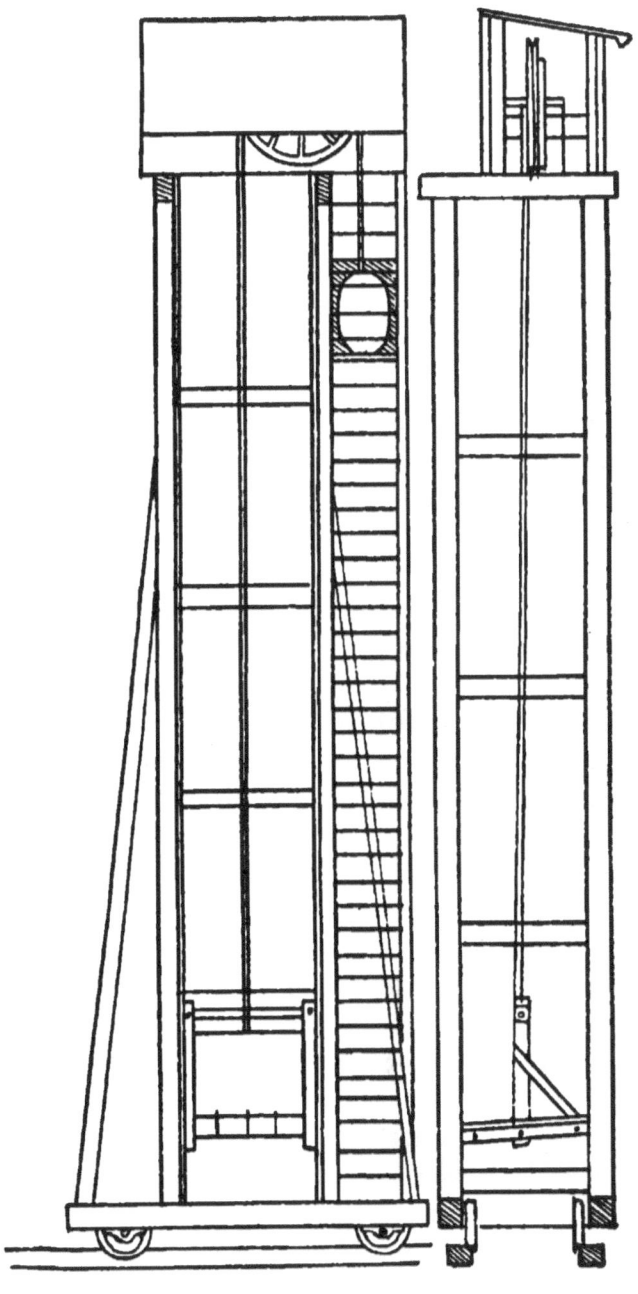

FIG. 58. LOWERING GIG AND TRACK.

and sawdust are also employed. When shipped to a distance, the floors and sides of the cars are lined, and in the South each cake is packed in sawdust and done up in burlap.

When shipments are made in vessels, runs are set up from the ice house, to discharge over the vessel's rail. As the distance is often considerable, the elevation of the runway is high near the house, and if the ice is taken from the bottom courses it is necessary, in some cases, to elevate the ice on to the vessel runway. The ice can be lowered into the hold with tongs. A gig, to take on two cakes at a time, handles the ice with great celerity, a counterweight returning the gig to the deck after the ice is discharged. Ice cakes are packed closely in the hold, being trimmed to shape, when required. Six or eight inches of sawdust are placed at the sides of the vessel, and, perhaps, ten inches of short shavings on top. Hay can be used, but sawdust is the best. Hatches are thoroughly caulked, and the hold is not opened until the end of the trip. The pumps must be sounded every day.

IN MARKETING ICE, painstaking supervision of details is constantly required. Resources should always be in efficient working order when required. A sudden hot spell often doubles the demand for ice, and the utmost exertions will hardly keep pace with it. Enterprise in extending trade should not be overlooked, and the efficiency of the service rendered is of special value in this direction. System and supervision should be extended through every department.

In retailing ice, as conducted in the large cities of the North, no detail of management is deemed trifling. Many ice dealers take pride in having neat and convenient wagons for their retail business. As a handsome wagon and a fine team are the means of attracting favorable attention, so there is nothing which causes more unfavorable comment than ill-kept stock and untidy wagons.

The quality of ice used for domestic purposes is now closely scrutinized, and cleanliness on the part of those handling this commodity, is expected. Ice wagons are usually

FIG. 59. A POPULAR ICE WAGON.

FIG. 60. ANOTHER ICE WAGON.

furnished with an ice scale, an ice axe, several pairs of ice tongs, an ice shave, a bucket, and sometimes a broom. The ice cakes are cut as required, cleaned, weighed, and placed within the customer's refrigerator or ice box.

The use of coupon tickets is a great convenience. The customer is furnished with a book at the beginning of the season, and for each delivery of ice he receives, a ticket is given back to the ice dealer. These tickets, having the name and quantity indorsed on them, avoid errors and disputes.

STRENGTH OF ICE.—Two inches in thickness of ice will usually bear up a man, four inches in thickness a horse, and ice five inches thick is generally safe for a team of horses and a loaded wagon weighing two tons.

Eight inches in thickness will bear up 150 pounds per square foot of surface, if distributed over an entire field.

Ten inches in thickness will support 250 pounds per square foot of surface. It is usual to estimate that ice eighteen inches thick will support a railway train.

WEIGHT OF ICE.—One cubic foot of ordinary ice will, on the average, weigh fifty-seven and one-quarter pounds, while a cubic foot of water weighs sixty-two and one-half pounds.

Thirty-six cubic feet of ice weigh 2,000 pounds. But as stored in the house, it is reckoned that forty-two to fifty cubic feet of space is required per ton of ice, depending upon the thickness of the ice and the care with which it has been cut and stored.

CHAPTER VI

THE USE OF ICE IN REFRIGERATION.

Cold Storage Ice Houses—Their Value for Handling Meats, Fruits and Vegetables—What They Will Do—Principles of Construction and Operation—How to Build Them—The Dairy and Cold Storage Houses—Convenience and Economy of Combining Them—Combined Ice House and Dairy —Very Cheap Ice Houses—How to Cut Ice in Small Quantities—Co-operation among Farmers to Secure Advantages of Ice Supplies.

THE USES OF REFRIGERATION are numerous in these days of invention and economy. The health, comfort and convenience of the civilized world are so intimately interwoven with results directly dependent upon the command, at will, of low temperature, that it is now of paramount importance to everyone.

Refrigeration in the commercial world is largely secured by mechanical means, and this method will receive notice in a later chapter. Cold storage, secured by ice, is in use all over this country, for domestic and trade purposes in preserving food products. The benefits of cold storage could be much more widely diffused, than at present, throughout all the farming communities, where ice forms naturally during the winter, adding materially to their profits and convenience, and an attempt is here made to show, in a practical way, how it can be secured.

THE CONSTRUCTION of a cold storage ice house, and the tools and methods employed for cutting and housing the ice, as well as the benefits to be secured, will be considered. Only such facts as have stood the test of practical experience, and which are within the limits usually attained by those who have good cold storage in use from year to year, will be presented. These results are only attainable by properly constructed storage houses, sufficient supply of ice, correct condition of articles when placed in cool room, length of time they are kept there and cleanliness. Cold storage houses, not built on correct principles, or improperly used, will prove of little account, and disappointment will follow their use.

Cold storage may be used to advantage in prolonging the market for many products. The entire crop, of fruit in par-

FIG. 61. A SIMPLE DELIVERY ICE WAGON.

ticular, need not be shipped at once, but by proper picking and storing shipping can be extended over several months.

Fresh meat can be enjoyed at will, and the lengthening of the season during which many varieties of vegetables and fruits can be kept fresh for the home table will not only add to the health and enjoyment of the family, but it is in the line of economy as well. Good health is the best doctor, and the more generous living which cold storage brings within reach is a precursor of health. In sickness a supply of ice and cooled viands is often beyond price. The suffering its judicious use may alleviate, and the numerous instances in which recovery is impossible without it, commend a supply of so beneficent a commodity to all. Ice is a necessity to health and comfort, and, as it can be readily secured in nearly all communities within the frost belt, very few farmers should be without it.

How Long Cold Storage will Preserve.—No rules as to the length of time during which various articles can be kept in cold storage to the best advantage, can be given, which will apply invariably to all cases. In stating what is often done in this way it is intended to show what it has been found profitable to do, and what will be likely to prove of practical value to those who are starting in to make use of cold storage for themselves. Poultry and fresh meats can be kept sweet for two or three weeks. Beef is improved in quality by keeping this length of time. Butter, eggs and lard may be stored for three to eight months. Apples, according to variety and condition, from five to ten months. Pears, pulled when they will just come away from the stem, and carefully handled, will keep two or three months. It is best to ship them in two or three weeks, not waiting for color to mature, as this will be perfected by the time they reach the consumer.

Concord grapes will keep two to four months in cold storage, and Catawba grapes will keep longer.

Strawberries, blackberries and cherries will keep two to four weeks.

Watermelons, three to six weeks.

Muskmelons, two to three weeks.

Peaches, four to six weeks.

Oranges, lemons, figs, bananas and raisins, two to three months.

Green corn, two to four weeks.

Squash, four to eight weeks.

Cabbage and turnips, eight to nine months.

Potatoes may be kept a long time; they have been kept, on a trial, several years, with no apparent loss of quality. Canned fruits will keep well, and ice cream can be conveniently stored.

The Temperature at which these results have been secured varied from 34° to 38° F. Bananas, oranges, lemons,

5

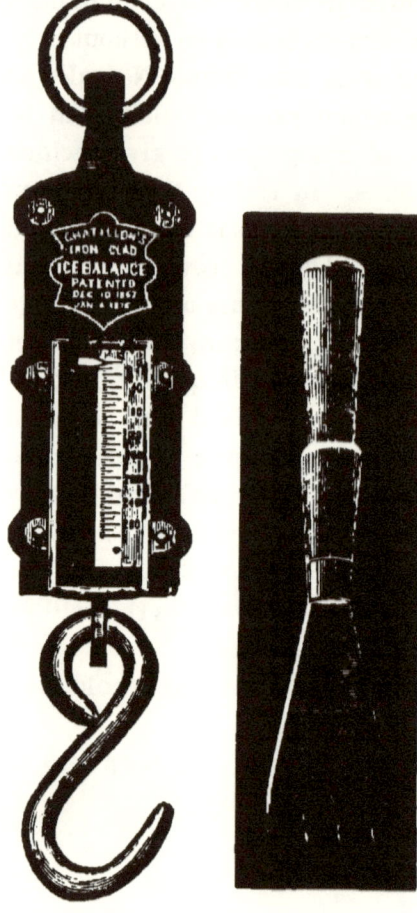

FIG. 64: WAGON AXE.

FIG. 62.   FIG. 63.   FIG. 65. WAGON SAW.

WAGON SCALE.   ICE SHAVE.

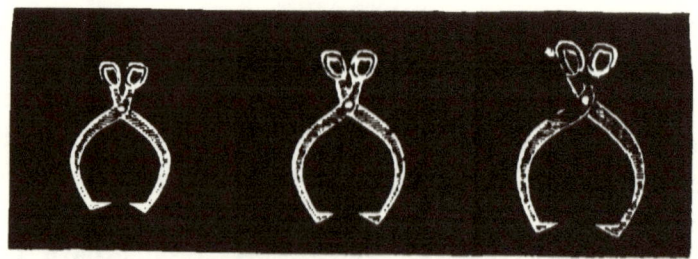

FIG. 66. WAGON ICE TONGS.

peaches, figs and raisins do better at 40°. Peaches, pears, berries, plums and all the more delicately flavored fruits keep in good form and appearance, but lose their delicate flavor if kept too long.

Fruits which are picked green, or before ripening, mature or ripen while stored. The tendency to decay in ripe fruits is arrested by refrigeration. Upon exposure to heat and air the usual process goes on more rapidly than in foods which have not been refrigerated. Food should enter into consumption with little delay when taken out of cold storage. The length of time during which it is desirable to keep goods in cold storage may be best determined practically with reference to the ends sought to be attained in any particular case.

THE PRINCIPLES OF COLD STORAGE.—Refrigeration depends upon the circulation of pure, dry cold air. It is based upon natural laws, which are well known and readily observed. Air exposed to heat is expanded in volume; it is thus made lighter and will rise, being forced upward by the surrounding cooler air. Air exposed to cold is condensed and made heavier; it will then gravitate to lower levels. The capacity of air for absorbing and retaining moisture varies with its temperature. Warm air will sustain a considerable amount of vapor, which will be condensed and precipitated if the air is cooled. As water is cooled and brought to the freezing point it expels a large part of the heat gathered at a higher temperature. As ice is melted to water this process is reversed, and heat and air are reabsorbed.

The operation of these natural laws is taken advantage of in refrigeration.

As usually constructed, cold storage ice houses are built with two stories; the first floor for storing goods, the second filled with ice. The floor between is arranged with openings, through which the air, chilled by contact with the ice, descends into the store room. A flue is provided to conduct the warm air to the upper part of the ice chamber, when it is dried and purified by contact with the ice as it descends on being chilled.

Drains and traps are required to carry off the meltage water, and to secure the water condensed from the warm air. Dampers in the cold and warm air flues assist in controlling the circulation, and ventilators placed in the roof keep the loft free from dampness.

The walls, ground floor and ceiling are constructed as nearly non-conducting of heat and cold as practicable. No cracks or any channels are permissible by which air can enter. Drains which take out the water are securely trapped, to keep out the air. Vestibules with perfectly fitting doors are placed at all entrances. Windows are fitted with three or four sashes and air spaces between.

Dryness in the storage room is secured by a sheet metal floor under the ice, usually galvanized iron, which forms a large pan or vessel, in which all meltage water is collected. Water is very destructive to the ice, and the warm air is kept away from the top of the ice ot prevent the moisture from being condensed there and settling on the ice. When the ice is low in the ice chamber, vapor may accumulate in the space above the ice. A ventilator in the top of the room is of service in conducting this away from the ice and keeping it dry. The water from the melted ice will absorb air and gases so it is spread out over as large a surface as practicable, and the air is conducted over it to be purified.

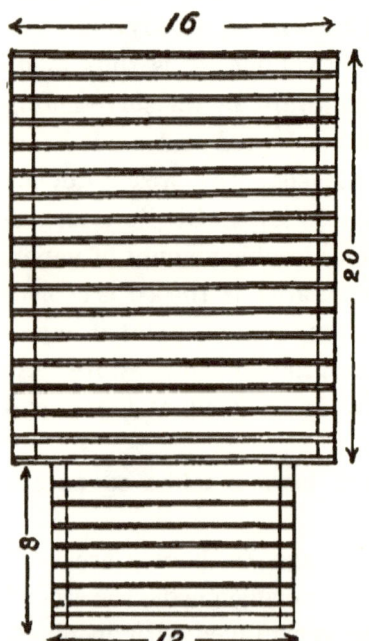

FIG. 67.   GROUND FLOOR.

There are several plans by which these general features are observed, in the construction of cold storage houses, some of which have been made the subject matter of patents.

The plans shown in the illustrations embrace the essential features of good cold storage construction.   These plans do not conflict with any patented devices, and will prove adequate for all practical purposes.

THE GENERAL ARRANGEMENT OF COLD STORAGE HOUSES may be, as shown in the illustrations, Figures 67-70, for any size.   Large houses require a girder and posts under the

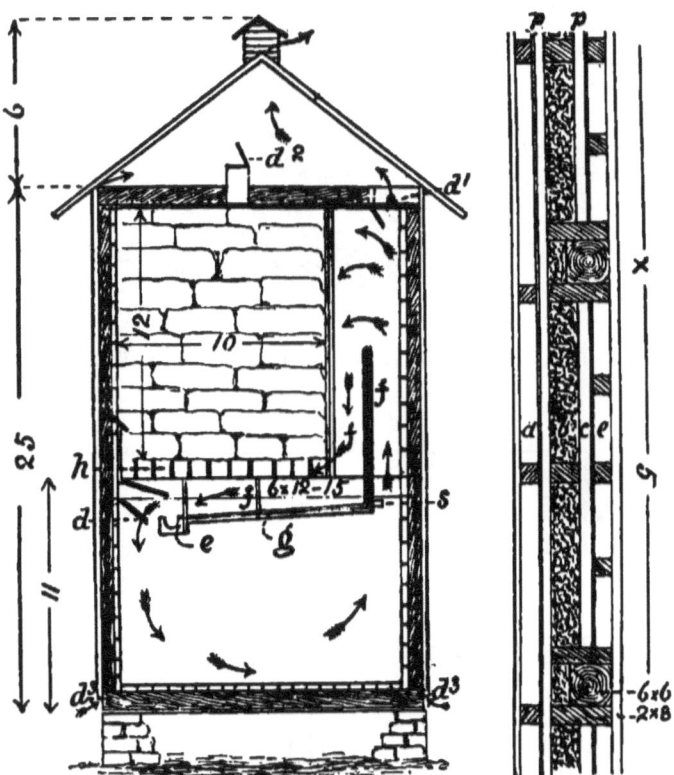

Fig. 68. Section of House.   Fig. 69. Section of Wall.
PRINCIPLES OF COLD STORAGE CONSTRUCTION.

center of the ice floor, and the air flues are best made double; one set at each side, with a drain on each side of the girder along the center of the room.   The construction of the walls vary.   Walls filled with sawdust, charcoal, tan bark or other 'non-conducting materials, have been in use for many years.

FIG. 70. EXTERIOR VIEW OF COLD STORAGE HOUSE.

FIG. 71. SECTION VIEW OF COMBINED ICE HOUSE AND DAIRY.

Carefully conducted tests, however, have conclusively proved that a wall of this description is inferior to a wall which contains dead air spaces, felt or paper linings, a section packed with mineral wool and an outer circulating air space.

The wall shown in Fig. 69 gives good satisfaction. It comprises air spaces, A, which are open to the outer air at the sill, and at the top open into the loft under the roof. Dampers D, in Fig. 68, are placed at the bottom, so they can be closed when desired. The next section, B, Fig. 69, is of dry sawdust, packed in place between walls of matched boards; the outer surface of these walls is lined with prepared water proof paper. The inner section, E, contains dead air spaces, which are about twelve inches square. The inner wall is of matched lumber and the outer one is of weather boards.

This construction keeps the sawdust dry, and the walls are free from dampness. The circulation of air through the outer air spaces carries off the heat imparted to the weather boards by the direct heat of the sun. When the air is humid, or charged with moisture, these air channels are tightly closed. The thickness of the walls may be varied with the capacity of the building. Additional sections of filling and dead air are required for large houses where large quantities of goods are refrigerated. Fig. 67 shows the ground floor.

The cold storage house shown in the illustration (Fig. 70) will hold forty tons of ice, and do all the work required for dairy, fruit and domestic service on a large farm with one filling of ice. By regulating the dampers, D D, Fig. 68, the circulation can be adjusted to meet all conditions. When these dampers are closed the ice wastes very slowly. The waste water, from meltage, is useful for cooling milk, and the milk room and cooling vats can be placed alongside the storage house or made a part of the same building to advantage.

A CREAMERY ICE HOUSE.—A very conveniently arranged and completely appointed creamery is shown in illustrations No. 72 and 73. Fig. 72 is a perspective view, and Fig. 73 the plan of a combined creamery, ice house and water tower.

The tank *B* is placed in the second story of the tower ; *C* is the ice house, *D* the creamery. At *I I* are set creamers, which are supplied with water from the tank by pipes passing through the ice house to cool the water. At *G* is a churn, which may be run by power located in the annex *E*. At *H* is a butter molder, and *J* is the veranda.

FIG. 72.   PERSPECTIVE VIEW OF CREAMERY.

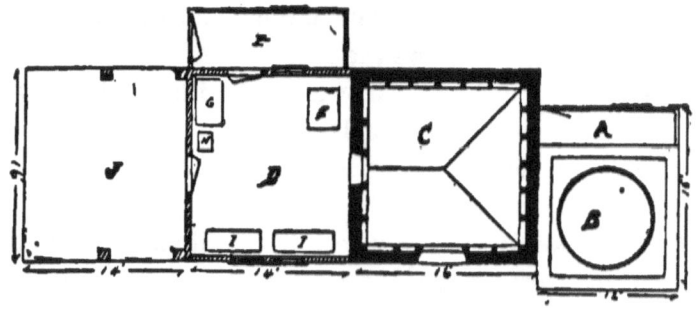

FIG. 73.   GROUND PLAN OF CREAMERY.

By raising the ice chamber, a cold store room can be secured below it. If the structure is placed on an elevation, water from the tank can be piped through the dwelling house.

COMBINED DAIRY, COLD STORAGE AND ICE HOUSE.—Such

an arrangement is shown in illustrations, Figs. 74 and 76. There is no communication between the dairy and storage room. For securing ice for the tank, double doors, made to fit very tight, are set in back of the ice chamber in the loft over the dairy. As leaving this door ajar would rapidly waste the ice, it should be under the care of a competent person and properly secured.

Where the ice house and dairy are required without the cold storage room, the plan shown in Fig. 71 is a good one. If a location on a sidehill is not conveniently at hand, the milk room floor may be excavated sufficiently to secure proper fall for drain. The floor of the ice house should be laid with hydraulic cement, and slope toward the end nearest the milk room. A cheaper floor is made from spent moulders' sand or coal ashes, mixed with enough lime to give a hard finish when dry. This makes a hard, durable floor. The water in the tank must be kept above the supply pipe from the ice house, to prevent any ingress of warm air. A trap placed in this pipe is a still better method. At L, Fig. 71, is a double door, through which ice can be taken out for the tank if required.

The size of these rooms can be taken at convenience. The ice house should not be less than twelve feet square and twelve feet high. Any smaller quantity than this wastes the ice much more rapidly. A house sixteen feet square and twelve feet high is a safe size for a dairy which is served by forty cows or less. The lumber for walls is better if matched, and the studding lined with paper. They are, however, often built from rough lumber, with no air spaces. The packed section should be ten inches in such cases.

A FREEZING HOUSE.—In some instances it is required to have a freezing temperature in the cold storage room. Poultry, dressed and frozen, and shipped in tight cases, has given good returns. This low temperature is secured by means of galvanized sheet iron tanks, Figs. 75, 77, 78, which are packed with broken ice and salt. From the surface of these tanks the cold is radiated directly into the room; hence, the larger the

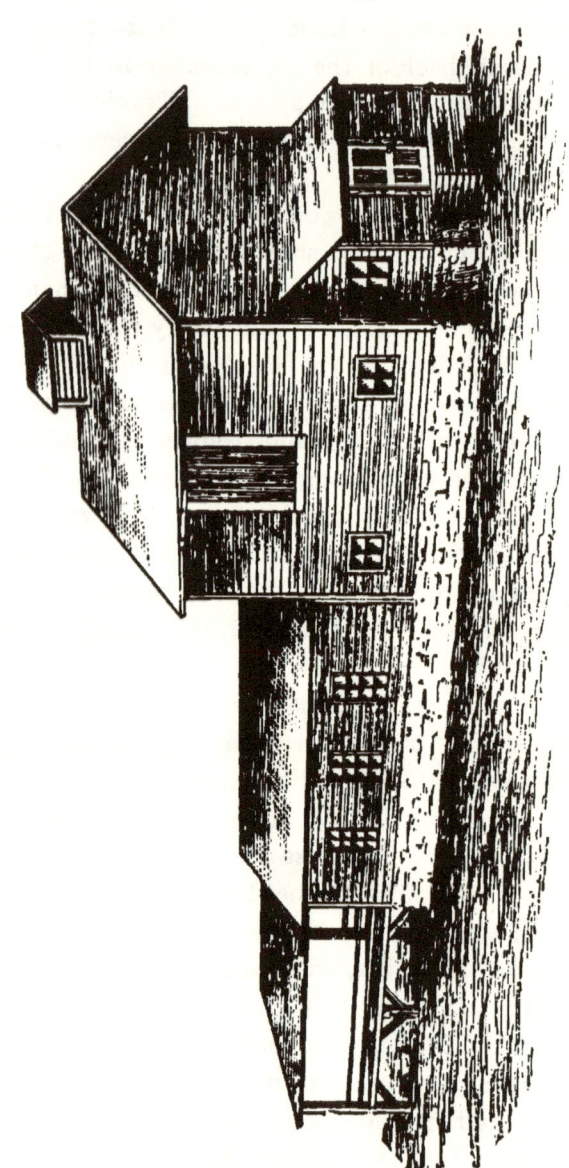

FIG 74.   COLD STORAGE HOUSE COMBINED WITH DAIRY.

surface of the tanks for a given capacity of ice and salt, the better, because of the large radiating surface.

The best form for the tanks is that of a hollow parallelogram. The lower edge should set about eighteen inches above the floor, to allow a circulation of air through the center of the tank. The tank should be a little wider at the bottom than at the top. This prevents the ice and salt from lodging. A tank six feet high, sixteen feet long, and three feet wide, placed at one side of the storage room shown in Fig. 68, and regularly supplied with ice and salt, will reduce the temperature of the room nearly to 0° F. As long as the supply of ice and salt is maintained, this low temperature can be held. The tanks are furnished with a trap to carry off the water, placed at the lowest end, and hand holds are arranged through which the salt which accumulates at the bottom may be

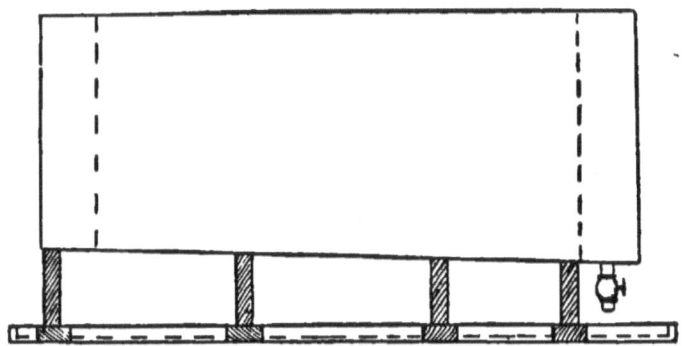

FIG. 75. SECTION OF REFRIGERATING TANK.

removed. A drip pan is set beneath the tanks to catch all drippings of condensation; these pans are of wood, lined with metal, and provided with a pipe to carry off the water.

Frost and ice accumulate on the surface of these cooling tanks, and their usefulness is thereby impaired. Duplicate tanks should be arranged, so that they may be used in turn, and the ice removed. The ice coat prevents the radiation of the cold into the room, and its force is spent in adding to the ice upon the sides of the tank, a useless waste.

In some instances the cold storage houses are divided into

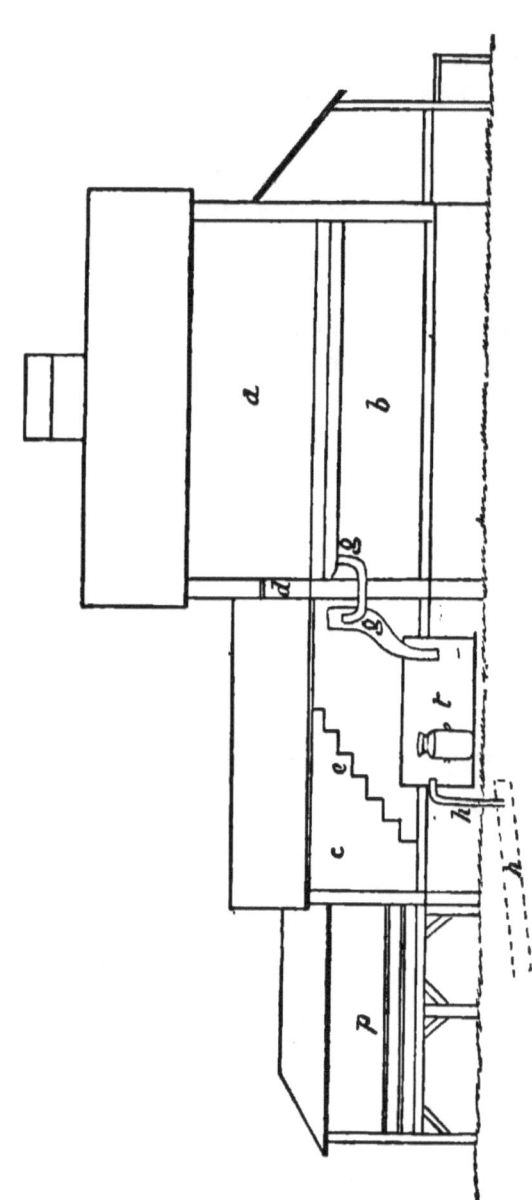

FIG. 76.   SECTION VIEW OF COLD STORAGE HOUSE AND DAIRY.

two or more rooms, so that various temperatures can be maintained to meet the requirements of a varied stock.

A VERY CHEAP ICE HOUSE, but constructed on the same principles as those laid down in Chapter IV for commercial ice houses, may take the form suggested by Figs. 79, 80, 81, or any desired modification thereof.

A STILL SIMPLER DEVICE.—Where the expense of an ice house is not warranted by the small use to which it may be

FIG. 77.   GROUND PLAN OF FREEZING TANK AND BENCH.

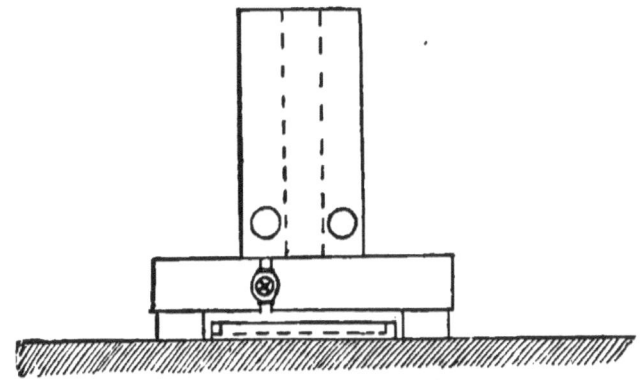

FIG. 78.   END VIEW OF FREEZING TANK.

put for cold storage, on some farms, a supply of ice sufficient for household purposes can be placed in any convenient corner of a barn or other building. A room partitioned off with rough lumber, and walls, as well as floor, well insulated with non-conducting filling, will answer, and repay its cost many times over during the summer. In Fig. 82 is a view of an ice room built into a corner of a barn in this manner.

An above-ground silo, if built of wood, with double walls and air spaces, will make a most excellent ice house, if provided with double doors. The underground, or masonry silo, should be boarded up, with joists between walls, and boards to form an air space, if used for ice.

A LITTLE ORGANIZED CO-OPERATION in any farming community where ice-cutting privileges exist, will secure an abundant supply of ice for all purposes for the entire section or neighborhood. It is customary to do the threshing in turn, and all participate in the use of the threshing machine and

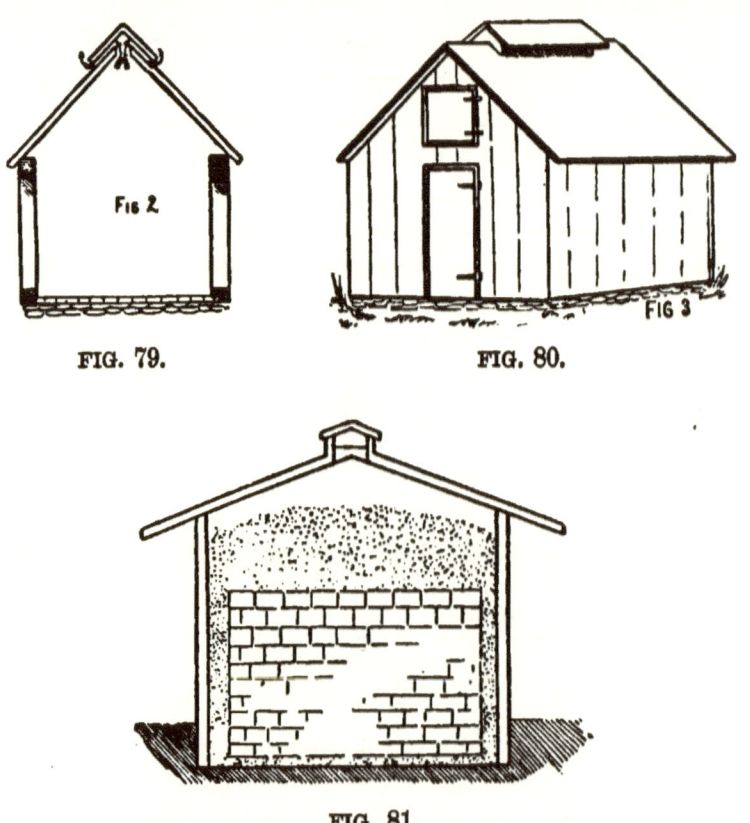

FIG. 79.　　　　　　　FIG. 80.

FIG. 81.

SUGGESTIONS FOR CHEAP ICE HOUSES.

power, where only very extensive farmers find it profitable to have an outfit for their own exclusive use.

In a similar manner the benefits of cold storage can be obtained. The houses can be owned by individuals, or by a few families who may be living near enough together to conveniently use one in common. The tools and outfit for cutting and handling the ice can be owned by a few enterprising young men, who can fill a large number of houses yearly by contract; or the appliances can be the joint property of all those having cold storage houses, who may combine to secure them, and also combine their labor in securing the ice crop. This work is done when the ordinary duties of the farm are light, and other interests would not be interfered with.

The practical advantages of this plan will readily present themselves to observing minds. An outfit of tools necessary to harvest, in good shape, one hundred tons of ice, will just as well harvest ten or fifteen times this quantity, and would really secure the larger quantity to better advantage than the smaller one. But, allowing that the labor in getting out one hundred tons of ice is the same

FIG. 82. BARN-CORNER ICE HOUSE.

per ton that it is for one thousand tons, the cost of the tools per ton of ice harvested is only one tenth as much in the latter case. The tools are durable, and will last many years. Ice plows which have been in use for fifteen or twenty years are still doing good service.

As the cold storage houses would be situated at several places, a brief outline of the methods in use for handling ice under similar circumstances, will be of interest. The ice is transported from the water to the houses by wagons or sleds. A platform is built near the edge of the water, in an easily accessible place, of a height a little above the bed of wagon boxes when they are backed up to the platform. The end of this platform is toward the water, and the teams are backed in on both sides. From the water end an inclined way or run is built down into the water. Upon this run the ice cakes are rapidly run up on the platform, quickly loaded on the wagons, and started on their way to the storage houses. Arriving at its destination, the load of ice may be deposited on the ground at the entrance of the house, and the team returned for another load. Meanwhile two men, with the assistance of a horse, can stow the first load in place in the ice chamber.

For such work the tools required on the ice field comprise:

One ice plow with guide.

One ice saw.

One ice chisel.

One ice floating hook, twelve to twenty feet long.

Three ice hooks, short lengths.

One jack grapple.

Two pairs of loading tongs.

At the ice house are required:

One pair hoisting tongs.

One pair drag tongs.

One pair edging tongs.

At this time the cash value of these tools is about sixty-five dollars for first-class goods, which are always the cheapest.

COST OF ICE IN THE HOUSE.—Regarding the cost of ice when stowed in place in the ice chamber, it would be difficult to quote an amount which would cover all cases. Locality and tact have much to do with determining this cost. Ice, twelve to sixteen inches thick, cut in small quantities and placed in the ice chamber, would cost, on an average, for labor, about fifty cents per ton. Where cut on a large scale the cost for labor in cutting and stowing is less than half of this amount.

A LOADING PLATFORM is illustrated in Fig. 83, which shows the method of running the ice cakes up with a jack grapple. The size of the platform is determined by the quantity of ice to be handled over it. One horse and grapple will readily serve several teams if a supply of ice cakes is maintained at the foot of the incline. Where many teams are to be served and the ice must be handled rapidly, two grapplers, one right

FIG. 83. A LOADING PLATFORM.

FIG. 84. EMBANKMENT PLATFORM.

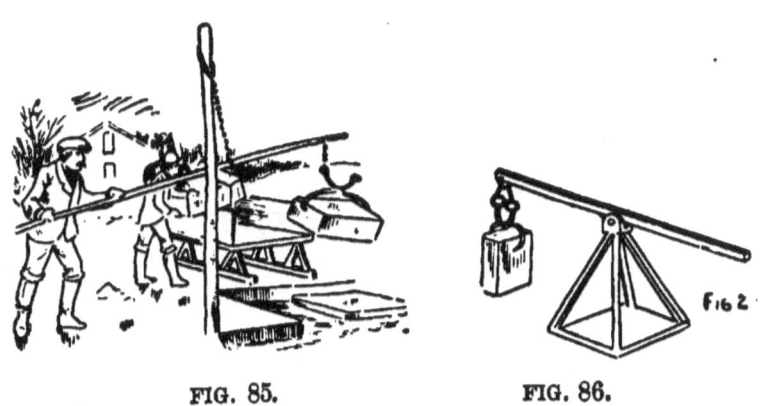

FIG. 85.   FIG. 86.

LIFTS FOR LOADING ICE INTO SLEDS.

and one left hand, can be used on the incline. By having the rope continuous and a pulling post at each end of the horse walk, the horse will pull a load each way, and several hundred tons of ice can be landed upon the platform in a day's run. Where the incline is long a team can be used to advantage on the grapple rope.

A sweep such as shown in Fig. 85 is a convenience in handling ice cakes directly from the water to sleds or wagons where only a small quantity is wanted, and where the ice platform is

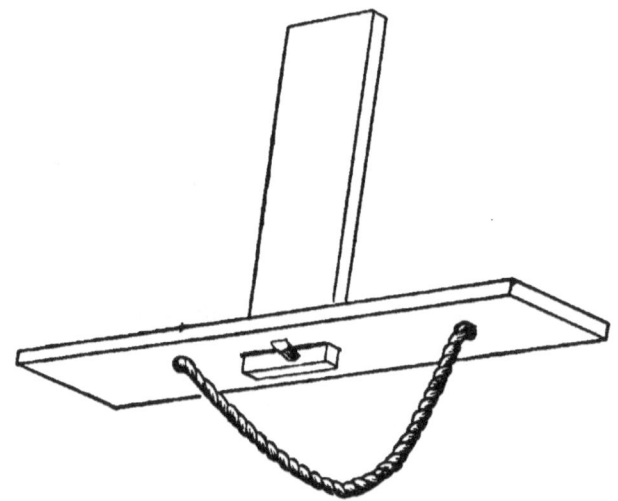

FIG. 87. A CHEAP ICE SCRAPER.

not required. A similar device, which has the advantage of being more readily moved, is shown at Fig. 86. Where an artificial pond is made with an embankment, a loading platform may be constructed, as shown in Fig. 84.

IN PACKING THE ICE into the ice chamber, attention is required to prevent any dirt from adhering to the ice and being packed into the ice chamber, where it will accumulate in the drains and on the floors as the ice melts.

At *S*, in Fig. 68, will be found an opening over the drip pan ; through these openings, placed at convenience along the back of the floor, the floor can be flushed with water and washed clean.

Time, labor and convenience are all conserved by the use of such necessary tools as are listed on previous pages. More can be added as the amount of ice cut is increased.

THE ICE FIELD should be kept free from snow by scraping from time to time. For clearing the small surface from which a harvest of forty tons can be secured, a simple scraper, cheaper than those used on large fields, will answer the purpose. An oak plank one and one-half inches thick, ten inches wide and six feet long, with two holes four inches from the bottom edge, and four feet apart, and a foot board mortised through the center, will do tolerable work. An iron shoe on the lower edge adds materially to its efficiency. Fig. 80 illustrates a scraper of this pattern.

Thirty-six cubic feet of ice weigh a ton. Hence, a surface six feet square on an ice field, where the ice is a foot thick, represent a ton of ice. At this rate a surface thirty-eight feet square would represent forty tons of ice. Owing to loss by breakage, and irregular cutting, it is usual to allow a considerable margin, greater in small than in large quantities, and a surface fifty feet square would readily harvest forty tons of twelve-inch ice. Where the ice is thinner a correspondingly larger surface is required to secure the same weight of ice.

The surface being cleared of snow, the ice plow is set upon the ice alongside a line drawn taut in the direction in which the plowing is to be done. The ice plow, drawn by hand and guided to run parallel with the line, gives the base groove. The blade of the guide is placed in this groove, and the field is now grooved in uniform spaces in one direction. The plow makes only one cut in each groove, while the guide is attached to it. By repeating this method grooves are made crossing those first made at right angles. The guide is now removed from the plow, and by plowing back and forth the ice is grooved to the depth desired, about seven or eight inches for twelve-inch ice and two inches for six-inch ice.

A channel is now opened at the foot of the incline, and a few hours work for four men, and a boy driving the horse to run the grapple, will land the ice cakes on the platform.

CHAPTER VII.

ARTIFICIAL ICE AND COLD AIR MACHINES.

Historical Sketch—The First Ice Machine—Its Subsequent Development—Progress in the Use of Machines—The Principles Involved in their Construction—Diversity of Application—Recent Discoveries.

The artificial production of cold has engaged attention from remote ages. The application of spontaneous evaporation in Eastern countries was the earliest method employed to produce ice.

America has the honor of being the home of the inventors who first achieved success in making artificial ice by modern methods. Jacob Perkins, in 1834, and Professor Twinning, of New Haven, Conn., in 1850, each procured British patents. The former did not procure a patent in this country, but Professor Twinning secured one in 1853. · Two years later, he had a machine in operation at Cleveland, Ohio, which produced 1,600 pounds of ice in twenty-four hours' run. This was a favorable result from a pioneer machine of an estimated capacity of 2,000 pounds in this time.

Much credit is due these early inventors, who introduced a type of machine which is now extensively employed, and is known as the compression system.

In 1851, Dr. John Gorrie, of New Orleans, La., patented a machine for producing ice, by compressing and expanding atmospheric air. This machine was also the pioneer of its class. It gave rise to what are known as air machines, used in England and on the Continent, and extensively employed for facilitating the transportation of fresh beef and mutton on the ocean.

In 1848, Ferdinand Carré, of France, contrived an original process for employing aqua ammonia. In 1865 he patented an ice machine, and at the French International Exposition, in 1867, daily produced six tons of ice. This has proved to be a notable invention, the present absorption system being based upon it and extensively used.

Efforts have been directed to expediting the spontaneous evaporation of water; a reduction of pressure being effected by a vacuum pump, and the vapors removed by a suitable absorbing medium. The utilization of cold obtained by the evaporation of other liquids, more volatile than water, have received attention.

There have been discovered a number of freezing mixtures, some of which produce wonderfully low temperatures. The addition of salt to broken ice is the best known of these; it is commonly employed in making ice creams and ices, and is of great commercial importance as applied to refrigerator cars and cold storage houses.

Of all these methods the compression, absorption and air machines, and the freezing mixture of ice and salt, have entered into commercial uses in this country. The details of the latter method are referred to in Chapter VI. Regarding the others, some account of the principal operations involved, and of the natural phenomena upon which they are based, will be given.

PRINCIPLES OF ICE MACHINES.—It has been observed of gases, that by compressing them to a fraction of their original volume, heat was produced. If the compression was great, most gases were liquified by it. A few gases were found which would not liquify, and were designated as permanent. By relieving the pressure, gases will resume their original bulk, and the heat of compression is gathered up or reabsorbed by them.

There is, naturally, a constant tendency toward the preservation of an equilibrium of temperature among the atoms of any body, and also between different bodies. This exchange is carried on upon a grand scale, in the economy of nature. Where the difference in degree is small the exchange is effected slowly, but where it is great the initial transfers proceed rapidly and with vigor.

By means of efficient insulation we can cut off, in a great measure, a room, or a part of a room, from the influence of the outer, or general exchanges of temperature. By this means we are able to bring this natural law into service, by controlling the exchanges of temperature of the objects we place in such rooms.

By the union of heat with a fluid, the latter is converted into a vapor, and the abstraction of heat from a gas converts it into a liquid. When a fluid or a gas is at the temperature at which a change in its condition is effected, the continued application or withdrawal of heat does not increase or diminish this temperature. This heat is termed latent, or hidden. The temperature at which ebullition takes place varies greatly with different liquids. Water boils at 212° F., while ammonia boils at 32° F. Some substances act as absorbents. Water will absorb about seven hundred times its bulk of ammonia gas when they are brought in contact.

In manufacturing low temperatures, by the Compression and Absorption systems, a liquifiable gas is used as the vehicle by which to impart cold to, and carry off heat from, the body to be cooled. Anhydrous-ammonia (ammonia from which all water has been removed) is usually employed. In the Compression machines, this gas is subjected to a pressure, averaging one hundred and fifty pounds per square inch, in a compression cylinder against a piston, which is operated by a steam engine. The heated gas is carried to a set of condenser coils, which are cooled by a water bath; here the gas is liquified by the reduction of temperature and the pressure. By this process it is made to part with the heat of compression, and its latent heat of vaporization, as well. The liquid ammonia is collected in a storage tank, and is then ready for refrigeration duty.

From this point the Compression and Absorption systems are practically identical. The liquid ammonia is allowed to escape through a valve with a minute opening, into what are termed the expansion coils. As the ammonia enters it is freed from about three-fourths of the pressure at which it has been held, and begins to boil and vaporize. As heat is necessary to accomplish this, everything within reach of its influence is placed under tribute. As the gas parted with about five hundred and seventy heat units per pound at the condenser, its capacity for heat is now very large.

The expansion coils may be placed in a loft of a cold storage room in the same position in which ice is placed for this duty. If they are submerged in a brine solution, the brine is cooled, and may be circulated in galvanized iron gutters suspended from the ceiling of the storage rooms.

After circulating through the expansion coils, the gas is drawn out and forced again into the compression cylinder by a pump which renders the system a continuous one.

In Making Artificial Ice, the expansion tubes may be submerged directly in the water which is to be frozen; the ice forms in huge cakes on the tubes, and is sawed into small cakes by a circular saw, when removed. This is termed the plate system.

In the can plan, a large tank holds the expansion tubes, and, suspended from its upper side, are numerous iron cans; a brine solution completely fills the tank, and, being chilled by the tubes, it gradually freezes the water which has been placed in the cans for this purpose.

In the Absorption System, aqua ammonia is placed in a retort containing a coil of steam pipes. A mixed vapor of water and ammonia is driven off, until sufficient pressure is developed in the retort to force the vapor through a small pipe into a condensing tank. Here the gas is cooled and liquified, and also rectified, or freed from water, making it anhydrous. The liquid passes into a receiving tank, and is then used for refrigerator work.

This duty is performed in the same manner as described for the compression machine. From the expansion coils the gas is returned to a tank called the absorber, where the water left behind at the condenser has also been sent; here they are reunited, and then pumped again into the retort, to begin the round anew.

IN THE AIR MACHINES, this gas is compressed in a cylinder against a piston, which is driven by a steam engine. The compressed air is cooled by water jets sprayed in the compression cylinder, and also in a cooling tank which has a water bath passed over it at the same time.

The condensed moisture is deposited in the cooling tank and in drying tubes, which are exposed to the spent air which has done refrigeration duty, and is still cool enough to further lower the temperature of the compressed air. After being dried, the air is expanded, producing an intense cold. This air can be circulated in tubes, or used for cooling brine, as in the methods already mentioned, or the air can be expanded directly into the storage rooms or ice tanks.

A LARGE PLANT FOR THE STORAGE OF FRUIT is situated at Waldo, Fla., and is controlled by the American ice and cold storage company. It is illustrated in Fig. 88. A perfectly dry, cool atmosphere is maintained, and a temperature so uniform as to demand only one degree of variation. The temperature at which the rooms have to be kept varies from 33° to 45° F.. depending on the character of the fruit which is to be stored. The higher temperatures are preferable, if sufficiently low to preserve the fruit. Retarding houses for keeping oranges or the more delicate fruits, can usually be more successfully managed by the use of refrigerating machinery, as it is not always possible to maintain a sufficiently even and low temperature by means of ice.

THE LATEST INVENTIONS.—All these ice-making and cold air machines are more or less expensive and complicated. It is natural, therefore, that inventors should be constantly seeking some plan, idea or method, for securing a low

FIG. 88. A FRUIT RETARDING HOUSE IN FLORIDA, WHICH USES REFRIGERATING MACHINERY.

temperature at less cost for the plant involved. The expense of the existing systems also prevents their use, except on a large scale; hence inventors are striving to find not only a method of producing cold at low cost, but one that can be adapted for use in houses, offices, stores, shops, cars, etc., on a more or less limited scale. Several devices for this purpose have already been patented. Some of them promise good results, though at this writing none seem to be thoroughly perfected. One of these devices employs a gas jet, or lamp light, the heat from which, acting on a kettle filled with chemical compound, produces a low temperature for a small house refrigerator, while the same principle is claimed to be applicable on a larger scale.

THE USES OF ARTIFICIAL REFRIGERATION are numerous. For cooling and ventilating buildings, aiding in some lines of manufactures, and in chemical works, it has proved its usefulness. In all hot climates it is extensively employed for making ice. In breweries it is applied very extensively, and is practically indispensable.

The handling of fresh meat, in the modern method, is directly dependent upon artificial refrigeration, and in no other direction are its benefits more marked or widespread. The cattle on our Western plains have become the daily food of those living at the antipodes. In ten years, from 1880 to 1891, the imports of fresh beef and mutton into Great Britain increased from 400 to nearly 3,300,000 carcasses. During the same period the exports of beef alone from the United States advanced from 50,500 tons to 101,500 tons.

Not only are meats carried in refrigerator vessels from America and the antipodes to England, but within a year Australian milk has been shipped in frozen blocks in such quantities as to be retailed in the streets of London for four cents per quart. Butter, cheese, eggs, fruits and other perishable products, are likewise transported enormous distances by rail or water, without injury to the quality, and at a low cost for freight.

It is also worthy of mention that refrigeration is now employed by the engineer, in substructure work in soils abounding in quicksands. A solid wall of earth is frozen and maintained in such soils, within which excavating and construction can proceed with ease and safety.

That many other uses for refrigeration will be developed goes without question. The students and inventors who are engaged on the problems involved in the production of artificial cold, claim that before many years all modern houses will be supplied with a refrigerating outfit in the garret to supply cold air to any of the rooms in summer, by gravity, as hot air is carried by flues from the furnace in winter. The universal application of a practical device for this purpose, will yield a rich reward for the successful inventor.

CHAPTER VIII.

ICE IN TRANSPORTATION.

Refrigerator Cars and Vessels—Value of Ice in Transporting and Marketing Perishable Produce—Ice and the Fisheries.

On all the important lines of railroads a regular refrigerator car service is maintained, for transporting perishable goods of all kinds. Butter, poultry, eggs, cheese, fruit, fresh meat, vegetables, and other articles, are despatched by this service. The shipping of packing-house products is an important branch of this department of railroad service, and a description of it will show the general features common to all branches of the business.

REFRIGERATOR CARS.—A cursory view of the cars in any freight yard discloses a decided difference in the appearance and thoroughness of construction among them. Those styled refrigerator cars fare very much better than their companions.

A critical examination shows that these cars are models in all
details of construction, and their finish casts the ordinary
freight cars far in the shade.

The main features of these cars are found, first, in their
walls, including floors and ceilings, which are variously made
of combinations of filled and air sections, with paper and felt
linings; second, an ice tank placed, sometimes at one, or both
ends, and in others in the roof of the car; third, in the regulation of the air supply, or ventilation. Some very elaborate
designs have been made, covering the features necessary to
the successful working of these cars. Most of them are
patented. The floor, ceiling and walls have several sections,
the outer being usually an air space, or a space filled with
thick hair felt. Following is a compartment filled with pul-
verized charcoal, or other non-conducting filling. This compartment is faced with carefully matched lumber lined with
paper. The walls are about six inches thick all together.

The doors are the same thickness as the walls, with bev-
eled edges, which wedge into the frame as the door is closed.
A fastening is used that is so made that a strong pressure is
brought against the door, forcing it into its seat, and an extra
precaution taken by inserting a strip of cotton flannel between
the door and frame, which thoroughly excludes air and dust.

In the best constructed cars there is no chance for direct
contact of the cooled air with the ice. This of special is
importance in cars in which fresh meat, butter, and other articles, are carried, which are absorbents.

Where the ice tank is located in the roof of the car, the
circulation of air is secured by gravity, and is changed by
admission of air through an opening so arranged that a
draft is created by the motion of the car. Very fine brass
wire cloth is doubled over these openings, to exclude the dust;
as the air enters, it is discharged against a water surface,
which catches the fine dust carried through the screens. The
waste water is discharged through a trap, which effectually
shuts off the entrance of air.

When the ice tanks are placed at the ends of the car gravity will not maintain a circulation of air. As the ice melts, the upper strata of air remains warm. To avoid this feature, resource is had in a forced draft. The air in the upper part of the car is collected by a fan and forced through tubes extending through the ice tanks and opening on to the floor of the car. In connection with the fan is an inlet and outlet tube, by which a gradual change of air is effected.

VENTILATING REFRIGERATOR CARS.—In some cars there is no provision for renewal of the air; the object is, no doubt, economy of ice, and for very low temperature, or for short trips, it is an advantage which does not have any ill effects on the contents of the car. For long trips and moderate temperatures, a change of air is beneficial, in most instances.

In some cars, ventilation is so arranged that the air can be changed or not, as desired. The fans are run by motion taken from one of the car axles, and are arranged to be run by hand when the car is not in motion.

ICING REFRIGERATOR CARS.—When a train is to be loaded with beef or mutton, it is set in on a track alongside of the icing platform. By means of double tracks on either side, as many as fifty cars can be iced at short notice. Ice cakes are delivered on a staging above the platform by elevator, suited to the location, and run into the hopper of a large power ice breaker. Barrows, of a capacity of five hundred pounds of broken ice, are set below the breaker, and, by withdrawing the damper, are filled with ice. From two to four shovelfuls of salt are added, and the barrow is dumped into the mouth of a chute which runs along the edge of the platform, delivering the ice directly into the door above the ice tank. About four tons of ice are placed in each car. By an extension spout the cars are filled in the same manner on the farther tracks. After icing, the cars are loaded, and at intervals on their journey the ice is replenished.

In shipping other goods, which are not wanted below the freezing point, ice is used without salt. Even with such goods, the more frequent use of ice would often be advisable.

VALUE OF ICE IN TRANSPORTATION.—It is difficult to imagine the state of affairs which would ensue upon a withdrawal of all refrigerator service upon our railways. The amount of privation and actual suffering which would follow would be felt directly in every community in the land. To most people the blessings which follow in the wake of the refrigerator car are of a kind which are accepted without question, as a matter of course. It would be a long list, to enumerate all the advantages which are now mutually divided between the producer and the consumer of the products of our farms, gardens, vineyards, dairies and fisheries, dependent, in whole or in part, upon this service.

It is but a short time since hundreds of bushels of fruit were left to decay on the ground in California orchards, while many other sections were destitute of fruit. Now a refrigerator car service delivers these fruits at all the Atlantic coast cities, as well as points between. Trial shipments have been despatched to London, with gratifying results, and it is more than probable that large quantities of the products of these famous orchards will delight our cousins across the sea.

REFRIGERATOR VESSELS.—On board the fastest steamships plying between our Atlantic ports and Europe, are found extensive refrigerator compartments. Dressed beef and mutton are exported in large quantities, as well as fruits, vegetables, dairy products and oysters. The temperature, for meat, is maintained a few degrees below the freezing point. Air machines are principally used on the ocean, the brisk circulation of air which they maintain being an advantage. The enormous quantities of dressed meat transported from the United States, Argentine, New Zealand and Australia, to Europe, requires a large fleet of steamers, some of which are equipped, at considerable expense, for this special service. In connection with these vessels, at both shipping and receiving wharfs, are large storehouses, where the frozen meat is held, awaiting shipment, or received after its voyage.

IN TRANSPORTING FRUIT ON THE OCEAN, a large fleet find employment; in it are found steamers built with insulated hulls formed by lining the outer steel hull with wood and packing the inclosed space with powdered charcoal. Refrigerator service is essential to success in transporting the more delicate fruits such as pears, peaches, cherries and plums which have been landed in London from California and South Africa in excellent condition in this way.

Ventilation, in connection with insulated hulls, is depended on in handling most of the tropical fruits imported into this country. Bananas from Central and South American and West India ports form the staple commodity, giving employment to an extensive fleet of very excellent boats. From Southern Europe large quantities of fruit are exported, oranges, lemons, grapes and nuts forming the bulk of the shipments which are carried in steamers in well ventilated compartments.

The development of the fruit traffic from different districts is attaining huge proportions with the control of the proper conditions for transit which shippers now have within their reach. Fruit shipments are now made to England from Florida and California, Southern Europe, South Africa and Australia. The shipments from one land forming the complement of those from others, a continual supply of the finest fresh fruits is available.

ICE IN THE FISHERIES.—It is now long ago that fresh fish were to be enjoyed only at places near by the fishing grounds. Now they are in the market the year round. During the season when fish may be caught, those not entering into immediate consumption are placed in cold storage rooms and frozen, to be taken out at any later time as they are wanted. Such storage houses are found in connection with all important fishing stations on the New England coast, along the great lakes, and among the salmon fisheries of the Northern Pacific. When the fishing boats start on a cruise they are loaded with ice, with which the fish are preserved, and the fishermen are not obliged to return home with a small catch to prevent its spoiling.

In shipping fish to inland places, a beautiful sight is often observed in a slab of crystal ice about three feet square and eight inches thick, within which a dozen or more fish have been frozen. They are as beautiful in appearance as when seen in their native element, while no occasion exists for commenting upon the utility of this method of transporting them. Altogether ice is a prime necessity in this business in all departments—the fisherman, the shipper and dealer, and the consumer.

It would not not do to close this chapter without referring to the oyster. The association of oysters and ice are so intimate that they are usually seen together. The trays of oysters and ice may be seen in every direction during the season, on their way from the oyster beds to delight the palates of their admirers who are found everywhere.

CHAPTER IX.

RETARDING CELLARS AND HOUSES.

Cold Storage in Modified Form, Without Ice—Ventilated Storeage and Packing Houses for Fruit and other Produce.

It is well known that cellars which are dry, cool and well ventilated are of great service in preserving fruit and vegetables. In Sicily, where oranges have long been produced in great quantities, they are kept in cool caves, which are numerous among the mountains of that island. Its volcanic origin no doubt has particularly favored their formation, and the porous nature of the rock insures ventilation combined with a dry cool air.

CAVES FOR STORAGE.—There is much of the natural phenomena of caves which is interesting, and definite determination of their philosophy would be of value. There are caves in which ice is formed during the hottest weather, and in which it disappears during the winter.

Shafts sunk in mining have exhibited the same peculiarity. The even temperature and dryness of the air in many caves is remarkable. While the facts are yet to be determined scientifically regarding these natural formations, some of their characteristics may be secured by artificially constructed cellars.

STORAGE CELLARS WITHOUT ICE have been in use for years, with profit and convenience to their owners. A convenient place is to locate them in the side of a slight hill, as shown in Fig. 89. A cross section is shown in Fig. 90. An excavation the width of the cellar is made, the earth being thrown up against the outside of the stone wall, which is built on the lower hillside. The opposite wall is formed by the cut face of

FIG. 89, PERSPECTIVE VIEW OF FRUIT CELLAR.

the hill. The rear end is constructed in the same manner as the lower hill-side. The front wall and doors are made of a double thickness of boards, with six inches inclosed space filled with sawdust.

The doors swing inward, and are large enough to admit a single horsecart. The sides and rear end are lined with inch boards. The side walls are four feet high in the clear. To form the roof, boards are cut of a length which will raise the center seven feet above the floor and give easy passage for a horse.

Midway between the center and either wall a 2x4 post is set upon a footing of brick, and above it under the roof boards a 1x4 strip is run the length of the cellar. On top of the first roof boards a layer of straw is placed, which will be a foot in thickness when pressed down.

On top of this straw a second set of roof boards is placed, covered with another layer of straw; on top is now placed a tight cover of matched boards, and two thicknesses of tarred paper over the whole. Battens are placed over the joints in the matched boards to hold down the tarred paper and prevent any water passing through. The outer edges of the roof are set firmly against the ground at the top of the walls.

On the upper hillside tiling should be placed, or other draining to carry off the surface water. A porous, gravelly side should be selected whenever available. In the front two windows are placed and one large one at the rear, double sashes being fitted during the coldest weather.

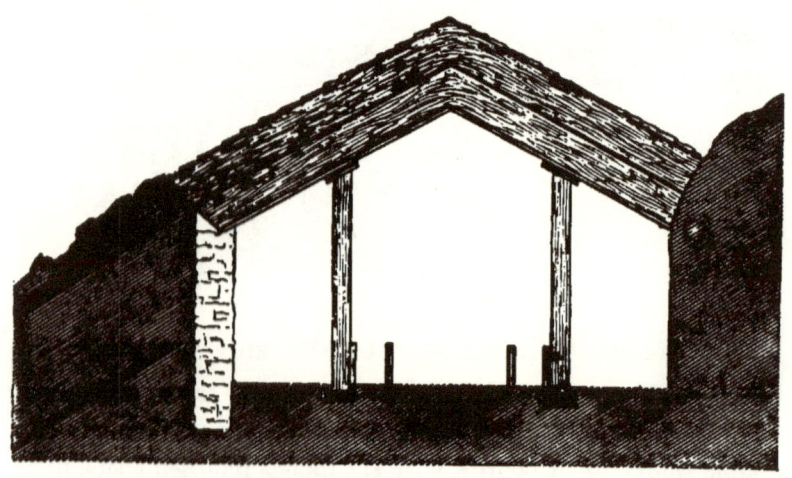

FIG. 90. CROSS SECTION OF FRUIT CELLAR.

THE CHEAPNESS AND CAPACITY OF SUCH A CELLAR.—For a cellar one hundred feet deep the estimated cost is $100, no skilled labor being required. Rough lumber is used except for the last roof boards. Large storage room is provided in such a cellar, fifty thousand celery plants have been accommodated in one; hundreds of bushels of vegetables, apples and other fruits have been held in it during the fall and winter.

A COLD PACKING HOUSE.—On large fruit farms a building designed to properly care for the fruit during shipping and packing, and as a store house for temporary use, is desirable.

The illustrations below (Figs. 91 and 92) are taken from a ventilated fruit house with insulated walls, which has operated very successfully in Ontario County, N. Y. A perspective view is shown in Fig. 91. The main building is 24 x 36 feet, built into a slight hill. The basement is built with stone walls eighteen inches thick, extending two feet below the surface and rising six feet above it.

The floor is made of eight inches of clean coarse gravel, with a coat of hydraulic cement grouted in a finishing coat on top, thus making a dry, hard floor.

The basement is divided into convenient apartments. The entrance is from the front and north sides, the floor being

FIG. 91. PERSPECTIVE VIEW OF FRUIT HOUSE.

almost level with the outside surface. Both the doors and windows are double, the latter being provided with screens to keep out insects when open for ventilation. This basement is ceiled with inch boards, on top of which, between the joists, is placed an inch and one-half of mortar.

The upper building is fourteen feet to the eaves, the main story being eight feet in the clear. The studding is five inches wide, and on the outside are two thicknesses of damp-proof paper, over which weather boards are placed. On the inside

of the studding are two layers of paper, then a two-inch wide
studding on which the paper is again doubled; over this comes
matched inch lumber, making two dead air spaces to insure
against the changes of outside temperature affecting that on
the inside.

The ceiling of this room is formed by putting one thickness of paper on the joists, covered with matched lumber.
The floor is of matched two-inch plank, thus making dead air
spaces between the cellars and the upper room, and also ren-
dering it impervious to rats and mice. (Fig. 92.)

This floor is occupied by an office and stairway in one end,
and these leave a clear floor space of 24 x 24 feet, for storing
and packing purposes. Shelves,
thirty-two inches deep, are placed
all around the wall of this room,
and are capable of holding about
seven tons of grapes or other
fruits, leaving the center for such
as are in barrels.

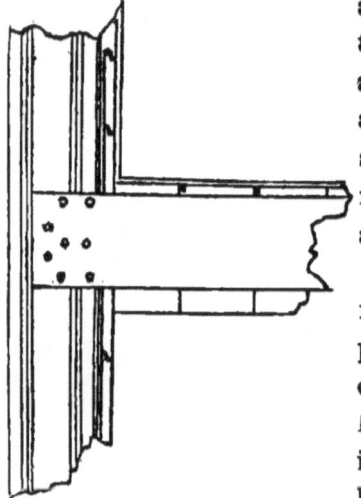

From the east side of this
room a door opens into the raised
portion of the shed. Through this
door the fruit can be unloaded
from the wagon without any lift-
ing. This shed runs the whole
length of the building and is six-

FIG. 92.   SECTION OF FLOOR teen feet wide, with a ground floor.
     AND CEILING.   It is ample to accommodate pack-
ing, also several loads of fruit over night or through a shower.

The top story is eight feet high in the center. The floor is
one-inch matched stuff, laid on paper. The sides and ceiling
are lathed and plastered. It makes a cool room, pleasant to
work in or to store grapes and other fruits in baskets, as the
veranda on the west side has a flat roof with a door opening on
it, which renders it very convenient for loading or unloading.
The veranda is six feet wide on the two sides.

A galvanized iron ventilating tube, two feet in diameter, runs from the fruit to above the roof, to carry off the heated air. Other ventilating doors should be close to the floor and left open at night, thus making a cool draft all night through the fruit room. The doors are to be closed air-tight early in the morning; the room above can be ventilated through the shaft all day, drawing off the heat from the roof.

Pure air and plenty of it being required in a house of this description, its location should be well chosen. The prevailing winds and surrounding buildings or other features can be noticed in selecting a site.

IN REMOVING FRUIT from storage room, it is always desirable to let the temperature gradually rise to that of the external atmosphere. Otherwise the fruit, being removed at once from a cool room, being cooler than the external atmosphere, condenses moisture on its surface which, unless removed, may cause decay after the fruit is packed for shipment or sale.

CHAPTER X.

ICED FOODS AND BEVERAGES.

Recipes for Iced Foods and Drinks—Ice Creams of every Sort and Description—Fruit Mashes, Sherbets and the like— Other Iced Dishes.

There are few who do not thoroughly enjoy a dish of well made ice cream or a glass of some refreshing iced beverage.

The addition of an ice house to the farm equipment is the connecting link which will supply these luxuries. Few entertainments are complete with ice cream omitted, and as it falls to the lot of the charming wives and daughters to dispense the cordial hospitality for which American farmers are famous, a few choice recipes are presented here for their consideration. The ice crusher illustrated in Fig. 93 is very convenient for breaking ice for the freezer or for iced drinks. It is an improvement over the common method of breaking the ice in a bag with a mallet.

Recipes for ices are not numerous, because many dainties are compounded by secret formulas for which confectioners sometimes have to pay dearly. Again, one who knows how to make good, plain, old-fashioned ice cream, generally knows how to add the different fruits and flavors. But the following have been compiled with great care, many of them are new or heretofore secret, and they are sufficient in number to give the housewife, caterer or confectioner every possible delicacy in the way of ices, exclusive of intoxicating drinks.

ICE CREAMS AND ICES.—Pour the mixture to be frozen into the tin can ; put beater in this and put on cover. Place in the tub, being careful to have the point on the bottom fit into the socket in the tub. Put on the cross piece, and turn the crank, to see that everything is right. Next comes the packing. Ice should be broken in large pieces, put into a canvas bag and pounded fine with a mallet, or put in a tub and shaved fine with the ice shaver. Put a thick layer of it into the tub, then a good layer of coarse salt ; continue this till the tub is full; pack down solid with paddle or common stick. After turning the crank a few times add more salt and ice, and pack down again, till the tub is full. For a gallon can three pints of salt and, perhaps, ten quarts of fine ice, will be required. The water must not be let off, as it is one of the strongest elements to help the freezing. If more salt than the quantity given is used the cream will freeze sooner, but will not be so smooth and rich as when less is used. Turn the crank for twenty minutes, not so fast at first, but very rapidly the last ten minutes. It will be hard to turn when the mixture is frozen. Let off the water carefully, turn back the cross-piece, wipe the salt and water from the cover, take off cover, not displacing the can itself. Remove the beater and scrape the cream from it. Work a large spoon up and down until the cream is light, and the space left by the beater is filled. Cover the can, cork up the hole from which the handle of the beater was taken, add more salt and ice till the can is well covered ; set in a cool place (covered with a bit of old carpet), until time for serving. It is better for standing a couple of hours. When ready to serve, dip the can for a few seconds in hot water, wipe it, and turn on a platter. Rest it for a moment, and lift a little. If the cream is to be served from a mould, remove it when you do the beater; fill the mould, and work the cream up and down with a spoon. This will press the cream into every part and lighten it. Cover the top of the mould with a thick white paper, put on tin cover, and bury in fresh salt and ice.

How to Serve Creams and Ices.—Much pride is taken by good cooks in the way they serve their dainties to their friends. Creams and ices look prettier served on pretty plates. If these are lacking, lay a flower on each plate, or in some way beautify it. A quaint way of serving cream was noticed not long since. Calla lilies had been robbed of their stamens and their cups filled with the cream.

ICE CREAMS.

Vanilla Ice Cream.—One quart of rich cream, one cup of milk, one cup of sugar, one and one-half teaspoonfuls of vanilla. This recipe nearly doubles itself if the cream is very rich.

Strawberry Ice Cream.—One quart of strawberries, one pint of sugar, one-half pint of milk, one and one-half pints of cream. Mash the berries and sugar together through a fine strainer into the freezer, after the rest of the mixture has been freezing about eight minutes.

Brown Bread Ice Cream.—Dry the crust of brown bread in a warm oven. Roll fine and sift. Add one pint of the crumbs to the preparation for vanilla ice cream. The vanilla and one-fourth of the sugar must be omitted.

Cocoanut Ice Cream.—One quart of cream, one pint of milk, three eggs, one and one-half cupfuls of sugar, one cupful of prepared cocoanut, the rind and juice of one lemon.

Beat together the eggs and grated rind and put with the milk in a double vessel. Stir till the mixture begins to thicken. Add the cocoanut and put away to cool. When cold add sugar, lemon juice and cream. Freeze.

FIG ICE CREAM.—One quart of milk, two tablespoonfuls of corn starch, one of gelatine, one pint of cream, a cupful and a half of sugar, three eggs, two cupfuls of figs cut fine, one tablespoonful of vanilla. Put the milk in a double boiler, reserving half a cupful. When it is boiling pour in the corn starch, which has been mixed with the cold milk. Cook ten minutes. Beat the eggs and sugar together; pour the cooked mixture on this, stirring all the time. Return to the fire, add the gelatine, which has been soaking in four tablespoonfuls of cold water, and cook three minutes. Set away to cool. When cold add the cream and vanilla, and freeze. When the cream has been freezing ten minutes, take off cover and stir in the figs. Cover again and finish freezing.

CHOCOLATE ICE CREAM.—One quart of cream, one pint of milk, one even pint of powdered sugar, one tablespoonful of vanilla, six eggs, one teacup grated chocolate. Mix sugar, chocolate, cream and milk, and bring to the boiling point in a porcelain kettle; then draw the kettle to the back of the stove, and stir in the mixture, six yolks and four whites, which have been beaten separately and together. Draw the kettle forward again, stir constantly till the mixture looks like thick cream, then take it from the stove and add the remaining whites, which have been well beaten. When slightly cooled add vanilla. When cold pour in freezer and freeze. This quantity is enough for twelve persons. Chocolate must be dissolved in a little boiling water.

NEW YORK ICE CREAM.—One full quart of cream, one coffee cup of powdered sugar, four eggs, three teaspoonfuls of vanilla. Beat the yolks and whites separately, then put together and stir in one pint of cream. When it reaches the boiling point draw cream to back of stove until the whole is well mixed, then draw forward, stir until it thickens, about three minutes. Cool, add the other pint of cream, then the vanilla. Freeze.

NEAPOLITAN CREAM.—Make a vanilla, a chocolate and a strawberry cream; freeze in separate freezers, and fill a mould the form of a brick in three smooth layers of equal size.

COFFEE ICE CREAM.—Make the same as vanilla, with the addition of coffee, of which take a cupful ground moderately fine, put over it just enough water to keep it simmering unti. strong, then pour through a bit of cheesecloth, and when cool into the cream ready for freezing.

WALNUT ICE CREAM.—One pint of the meat of walnuts (American are the best), pounded fine in a mortar, one pint of milk, one quart of cream, two small cupfuls of sugar, four eggs and a quarter of a teaspoonful of salt. Beat eggs with

FIG. 93.   ICE CRUSHING MACHINE.

one cupful of sugar; put them and the milk into double boiler and stir constantly until the mixture begins to thicken. Then add salt and put away to cool. When cold add the rest of the sugar, cream and nut meats, and freeze.

TEA ICE CREAM.—One and one-half pints of rich cream, one pint of sugar, one cup of good strong green tea, yolks of eight eggs. Mix in inner vessel until it thickens. Strain through sieve and freeze.

ORANGE ICE CREAM.—One and one-half pints of milk or cream. One pint of sugar. The rind of two oranges rubbed on loaf sugar. The juice of six large oranges. Yolks of eight eggs. A pinch of salt. Mix the ingredients in an inner vessel. Stir well until the mixture thickens. Pass through fine sieve. Freeze.

CINNAMON ICE CREAM.—One and one-half pints of rich cream. One pint of sugar. Yolks of eight eggs. A good sized stick of cinnamon, bruised. Cook in inner vessel until mixture thickens. Strain, cool and freeze.

VANILLA ICE CREAM.—One and one-half pints cream. One pint of sugar. One vanilla bean. Yolks of seven eggs, and a pinch of salt. Break up the bean in the mixture, and proceed as in Cinnamon Cream.

ALMOND CREAM.—One pint of cream. One cup of sugar. One-quarter pound of blanched almonds, well chopped. Stir over fire, and add well beaten yolks of four eggs. Flavor with extract of rose. Pour into dish and pile on meringue. Place on ice until time to serve.

TAPIOCA CREAM.—Soak two tablespoonfuls of tapioca over night in just enough water to cover it. In the morning boil one quart of milk with the soaked tapioca by placing it in a tin can or pail set in water to boil. Add two-thirds of a cup of granulated sugar and a pinch of salt. Beat the yolks of three eggs. When the milk has boiled eight minutes stir in the yolks. Remove from the fire and stir rapidly for five minutes, so that it will not curdle. Flavor with vanilla. Pour into pudding dish. Beat whites well. Pour over the top of cream. Sift with a little powdered sugar, brown a minute or two in oven. Serve ice cold.

SWANS' DOWN CREAM.—Whip stiff one pint of rich cream. Beat to a froth the whites of three eggs; sweeten with a small cup of sugar and flavor with vanilla. Beat all together. Pour into a glass dish and set into a bowl of crushed ice to send to table. Eat with sponge cake.

PEACH ICE CREAM.—One quart of cream. One cup of milk sweetened. Whites of three eggs. One pint of sliced peaches.

As soon as the cream begins to freeze well add the sweetened peaches which have been run through a sieve. Freeze seven minutes and add the beaten whites. Freeze well.

ICED DISHES.

LEMON ICE.—Eight lemons, two quarts of water, one and one-half pounds of sugar, whites of four eggs. This makes three quarts to freeze.

TUTTI FRUTTI.—When rich vanilla cream is partly frozen add English currants, chopped citron, chopped raisins and candied cherries. The rule is generally the same quantity of fruit as cream. Mould and place in pounded ice and salt until ready to serve. A sufficient time must be allowed for the cream to harden. Blanched almonds chopped fine makes a nice addition.

FROZEN PUDDING.—One generous pint of milk, two cupfuls of granulated sugar, a scant half cupful of flour, two eggs, two tablespoonfuls of gelatine, one quart of cream, one pound of French candied fruit (half a pound will do), four tablespoonl fuls of wine. Let the milk come to a boil, beat the flour, one cupful of sugar and the eggs, and stir into the boiling milk. Cook twenty minutes, and add the gelatine, which has been soaking an hour in enough water to cover it. Set away to cool. When cold, add wine, sugar and cream. Freeze ten minutes, then add the candied fruit and finish freezing. When ready to serve dip tin in warm water, turn out the cream and serve with whipped cream heaped around.

NESSELRODE PUDDING.—One pint of shelled almonds, one pint and a half of shelled chestnuts, one pint of cream, a pint can of pineapple, the yolks of ten eggs, half a pound of French candied fruit, one tablespoonful of vanilla, four of wine, one pint of water, one of sugar. Boil the chestnuts half an hour, then rub off the black skins and pound in a mortar until a paste. Blanch the almonds and pound in same manner. Boil the sugar, water and juice from the pineapple for twenty minutes in a saucepan. Beat the yolks of the eggs and stir them into the syrup. Put the saucepan in another of boiling water, and beat the mixture with an egg beater until it thickens. Take off, place in basin of cold water, and beat ten minutes. Mix the almonds and chestnuts with the cream, and rub all through a sieve. Add the candied fruit and pineapple cut fine; mix this with cooked mixture; add the flavor and half a a teaspoonful of salt. Freeze the same as ice cream.

LEMON SHERBET.—The juice of five lemons, one pint of water, one tablespoonful of gelatine. Soak the gelatine in a little water. Boil one cup of water and dissolve the gelatine in it. Mix together the sugar, water, gelatine and lemon juice. Turn into can and freeze. This is light and creamy.

LEMON SHERBET.—One pint and a half of sugar, three pints of water, the juice of ten lemons. Boil the sugar and water together twenty-five minutes. Add the lemon-juice, strain and freeze. This makes a smooth, rich sherbet.

ORANGE SHERBET.—Make the same as lemon sherbet, but use the juice of twenty oranges instead of ten lemons. Boil the syrup for this dish thirty minutes.

PINEAPPLE SHERBET.—A pint and a half can of pineapple, or, if fresh fruit is used, one large pineapple, a scant pint of sugar, a pint of water, one tablespoonful of gelatine. Soak the gelatine an hour in enough cold water to cover it. Cut the hearts and eyes from the fruit, chop it fine and add to it the sugar and juice from the can. Have half the water hot and dissolve the gelatine in it. Stir this and the cold water into the pineapple. Freeze. This sherbet will be white and creamy.

STRAWBERRY SHERBET.—Two quarts of strawberries, one pint of sugar. one pint and a half of water, one tablespoonful of gelatine. Mash the berries and sugar together, and let them stand two hours. Soak the gelatine in cold water to cover. Add one pint of water to the berries, and strain. Dissolve the gelatine in half a pint of boiling water; add this to the strained mixture, and freeze.

STRAWBERRY SHERBET No. 2.—One pint and a half of

strawberry juice, one pint of sugar, one pint and a half of water, the juice of two lemons. Boil the water and sugar together for twenty minutes, add the lemon and strawberry juice. Strain and freeze.

RASPBERRY SHERBET.—This sherbet is made the same as the strawberry. When raspberries are not in season, use the canned or preserved fruit and a smaller quantity of sugar. The juice of a lemon or two is always an improvement. This sherbet can also be made by following the second rule for strawberry sherbet.

CURRANT SHERBET.—One pint of currant juice, one pint and a half of water, the juice of one lemon, one pint of sugar, one tablespoonful of gelatine. Have the gelatine soaked in cold water and dissolve it in half a pint of boiling water. Mix it with the pint of cold water, the sugar, lemon and currant juice, and freeze.

FROZEN STRAWBERRIES.—Two quarts of fresh berries, one pint of sugar, one quart of water. Boil the water and sugar together half an hour, then add the berries, and cook fifteen minutes longer. Let this cool, and freeze. When beater is taken out add one pint of whipped cream. Preserved fruit may be used in this case, to each quart of fruit one quart of water, and freeze.

FROZEN RASPBERRIES.—Prepare raspberries the same as strawberries. When cold add the juice of three lemons, and freeze.

FROZEN APRICOTS.—One can of apricots, a generous pint of sugar, a quart of water, a pint of whipped cream—measured after being whipped. Cut apricots in small pieces, add sugar and water, freeze.

FROZEN PEACHES.—One can of peaches, one heaping pint of granulated sugar, one quart of water, two cupfuls of whipped cream. Boil sugar and water together for twenty minutes, then add peaches, and cook twenty minutes longer. Rub through a sieve, and when cool, freeze. When the beater is taken out stir in the whipped cream with a spoon.

BISCUIT GLACE.—One pint of cream whipped to a froth, a dozen and a half macaroons, three eggs, half a cupful of water, two-thirds of a cupful of sugar, a teaspoonful of vanilla. Boil the sugar and water together for half an hour, beat the eggs and stir into the boiling syrup. Place the saucepan containing the mixture in another of boiling water, and beat for eight minutes. Take from the fire, place the saucepan in a pan of cold water, and beat mixture until cold. Then add flavor and whipped cream. Stir well and fill paper cases. Have the macaroons rolled fine and browned. Put a layer of crumbs on the cream in the cases. Place these in an ice cream mould, cover well and bury in ice and salt for at least two hours. Serve on fancy plates.

GLACE MERINGUE.—One quart of cream, one large cupful of granulated sugar and six tablespoonfuls of powdered, one tablespoonful of vanilla, the whites of six eggs, one cupful of milk, one tablespoonful of gelatine, soaked an hour in four of cold water. Let the milk come to a boil, and stir the gelatine into it. Strain into the cream, add the vanilla and granulated sugar; turn into the tin and freeze. When the mixture is frozen (it will usually require twenty minutes), take out the beater and pack the cream smoothly, being careful to have the top perfectly smooth. Set away until serving time. It should stand, at least, an hour. When ready to serve, beat the whites of the eggs to a stiff froth, and gradually beat into this the powdered sugar. Turn the cream out, and cover every part of it with the meringue. Brown in a hot oven and serve immediately. If the dish is flat put a board under it; this keeps the heat from the bottom. Glace meringue is a beautiful dish.

BOMBE GLACE.—One quart of strawberry or raspberry sherbet, one pint of sugar, one pint and a half of water, the yolks of eighteen eggs, one large tablespoonful of vanilla. Boil the sugar and water together twenty minutes, beat the yolks of the eggs very light. Place the saucepan with the syrup in another pan of boiling water; stir the eggs into this syrup and beat with a whisk for ten minutes. Take from the fire, place the basin in a pan of cold water, and continue beating for ten or fifteen minutes. Pack an ice cream mould in ice and salt. Take the sherbet from the freezer and spread on the sides and bottom of the mould. When it is hard put the cooked mixture in the center, being careful not to disturb the sherbet. Cover with a piece of thick white paper. Put on the cover, and cover the top of the mould with salt and ice. Bombe glace can be made with any kind of sherbet, having

FIG. 94. A POWER ICE CRUSHER.

the center part flavored to correspond with the sherbet. The handsomest dishes are, of course, made with the brightest colored sherbets.

PLAIN BLANC MANGE.—To one quart of boiling milk add two tablespoonfuls of corn starch dissolved in a little cold milk. Sweeten and let it boil long enough to thicken. Pour into cups, and when cold serve in glass dishes with a sweet jelly and rich cream. This makes a very simple and wholesome dish.

Always cook custards in inner vessels, as they are not so apt to scorch. A frozen custard is a delight in hot weather.

PINEAPPLE WATER ICE.—One pound of pineapple, peeled, sliced and reduced to a pulp by pounding. Rub through a fine sieve. Wash the dregs with half pint of cold water. Add one pint of syrup (made by boiling one pint of water with quarter of a pound of sugar) and juice of one lemon. Freeze.

RASPBERRY ICE.—One and one-half pints of raspberry juice, made by pressing the fruit through a sieve. One pint of syrup. One glass of currant juice, or juice of half a lemon. Freeze.

CHERRY ICE.—Two pounds of cherries picked, pounded and boiled with a gill of water in a porcelain vessel. Rub through a sieve. Add one pint of thick syrup, one pint of cream, and a few drops of essence of the kernels. Mix. Freeze twenty minutes.

BLACKBERRY ICE.—Put as many blackberries as you wish to stew, and sweeten to taste. When done put in a bag and strain. When cold, freeze.

MACARONI CUSTARD. — Take one quart of milk, set it on to boil. Mix one-half tablespoonful of butter and three of flour, and stir into the boiling milk. Beat the yolks of six eggs with one-half cup of sugar. Stir into the milk, and take from fire to cool. Flavor with vanilla, then crumble one dozen fresh macaroons over the top and pile on the meringue. Serve ice-cold.

BOILED CUSTARD.—One quart of milk, two eggs, one tablespoonful of corn starch, one teacup of sugar. Flavor with vanilla. Boil milk and sugar, then add starch and eggs well beaten together. Place on ice before serving.

FLOATING ISLAND.—One quart of milk, four eggs—whites and yolks beaten separately—four tablespoonfuls of sugar, two teaspoonfuls vanilla, one-half cup of currant jelly. Heat the milk to scalding, but not boiling. Beat the yolks, stir into them the sugar and pour upon them gradually, mixing well a cup of hot milk. Return to saucepan and boil until it begins to thicken. Pour into glass dish. Heap upon the top meringue of whites whipped very stiff, into which you have beaten the jelly, a teaspoonful at a time. Serve ice cold.

BLANC MANGE.—Sweeten one quart of cream and flavor to suit the taste. Dissolve one tablespoon of gelatine in hot water and pour into the cream. Set on ice and serve with whipped cream.

CORN STARCH BLANC MANGE.—Dissolve three tablespoonfuls of corn starch in one pint of milk. Add three teaspoonfuls of sugar and three beaten eggs. Put this mixture into a pint of boiling milk. Flavor to taste. Pour into cup. Serve with jelly and whipped cream.

VELVET BLANC MANGE.—Two cups of sweet cream. One-half cup of gelatine dissolved in hot water. One-half cup of powdered sugar. One small glass of white wine. Flavor with almond extract. Boil cream, sugar and gelatine until it is smooth, then take it from the fire and flavor by adding the wine last. Stir well and put in fancy mould on ice. Serve with cream.

LEMON JELLY.—To a package of gelatine add one pint of cold water and the juice of four lemons. In an hour it will be sufficiently dissolved to add a pint of boiling water and three scant cups of sugar. Let it just come to a boil. Strain through cheese cloth into fancy moulds. Set on ice, and serve with rich cream.

STRAWBERRY ICE.—Crush three quarts of strawberries with two and one-half pounds of sugar. Let them stand an hour. Squeeze through a straining bag. Add an equal amount of water to the juice, and when half frozen add the beaten whites of three eggs. Any juicy fruit may be prepared in the same manner, currants and raspberries being especially good.

SNOW PUDDING.—Dissolve in one pint of boiling water half a box of good gelatine. When cold add juice of one lemon and small cup of sugar. Strain well and add the well beaten whites of three eggs. Mix well and pour into mould. When ice-cold serve with a custard made of the yolks of eggs and a pint of cream or milk. Sweeten and flavor to taste.

8

ICED COFFEE.—One quart of strong coffee, one quart of cream, one and three-fourths of a pint of granulated sugar. Freeze.

ICED TEAS are now served to considerable extent during warm weather. They are used without milk, and the addition of sugar serves only to destroy the finer tea flavor. It may be prepared early in the day, taking care to make it stronger than when served hot. Place in refrigerator, and when ready to serve, have crushed ice in the tumblers, which are nicer for the purpose than cups, as the tea looks pretty poured through the ice.

LEMONADE.—Juice of half a lemon to each goblet of water. Sweeten to taste and pour over crushed ice.

JELLY WATER.—Sour jellies dissolved in water make delicious drinks for fever patients. Best always to boil the jelly in water, then cool. In this way the jelly does not become lumpy.

A COOLING DRINK.—Pour three quarts of water on an ounce of cream of tartar. Stir in it the juice of a fresh lemon and the peel cut in very thin strips without a particle of pulp. Sweeten to taste. Let stand till cold and clear. Pour off without disturbing sediment at the bottom. A tumblerful iced is a pleasant and healthful beverage for a warm day.

EGG LEMONADE.—White of an egg, juice of one lemon, one tablespoonful sugar, one tumbler of water. Beat well together. Serve cold.

GUM ARABIC WATER.—One teaspoonful gum arabic. One tumbler cold water. Allow it to stand long enough to dissolve. Flavor with jelly, lemon, or any fruit syrup.

SAGO MILK.—Three tablespoonfuls sago, soaked in a cup of cold water one hour. Add three cups of boiling milk. Sweeten and flavor to suit taste. Simmer slowly half an hour. Eat warm. Tapioca milk is prepared in the same manner.

LIST OF ILLUSTRATIONS.

115

INDEX.

Mushrooms. How to Grow Them.

For home use fresh Mushrooms are a delicious, highly nutritious and wholesome delicacy; and for market they are less bulky than eggs, and, when properly handled, no crop is more remunerative. Anyone who has an ordinary house cellar, woodshed, or barn can grow Mushrooms. This is the most practical work on the subject ever written, and the only book on growing Mushrooms ever published in America. The whole subject is treated in detail, minutely and plainly, as only a practical man, actively engaged in Mushroom growing, can handle it. The author describes how he himself grows Mushrooms, and how they are grown for profit by the leading market gardeners, and for home use by the most successful private growers. The book is amply and pointedly illustrated, with engravings drawn from nature expressly for this work. By Wm. Falconer. Is nicely printed and bound in cloth. Price, post-paid_____ 1.50

Allen's New American Farm Book.

The very best work on the subject; comprising all that can be condensed into an available volume. Originally by Richard L. Allen. Revised and greatly enlarged by Lewis F. Allen. Cloth, 12mo... 2.50

Henderson's Gardening for Profit.

By Peter Henderson. New edition. Entirely rewritten and greatly enlarged. The standard work on Market and Family Gardening. The successful experience of the author for more than thirty years, and his willingness to tell, as he does in this work, the secret of his success for the benefit of others, enables him to give most valuable information. The book is profusely illustrated. Cloth, 12mo.,.. 2.00

Fuller's Practical Forestry.

A Treatise on the Propagation, Planting, and Cultivation, with a description and the botanical and proper names of all the indigenous trees of the United States, both Evergreen and Deciduous, with Notes on a large number of the most valuable Exotic Species. By Andrew S. Fuller, author of "Grape Culturist," "Small Fruit Culturist," etc. 1.50

The Dairyman's Manual.

By Henry Stewart, author of "The Shepherd's Manual," "Irrigation," etc. A useful and practical work by a writer who is well known as thoroughly familiar with the subject of which he writes. Cloth, 12mo_____ 2.00

Truck Farming at the South.

A work giving the experience of a successful grower of vegetables or "grain truck" for Northern markets. Essential to any one who contemplates entering this promising field of Agriculture. By A. Oemler, of Georgia. Illustrated. Cloth, 12mo_____ 1.50

Harris on the Pig.

New edition. Revised and enlarged by the author. The points of the various English and American breeds are thoroughly discussed, and the great advantage of using thoroughbred males clearly shown. The work is equally valuable to the farmer who keeps but few pigs, and to the breeder on an extensive scale. By Joseph Harris. Illustrated. Cloth, 12mo _____ 1.50

Jones's Peanut Plant—Its Cultivation and Uses.

A practical Book, instructing the beginner how to raise good crops of Peanuts. By B. W. Jones, Surry Co., Va. Paper Cover,.... .50

Barry's Fruit Garden.

By P. Barry. A standard work on fruit and fruit-trees; the author having had over thirty years' practical experience at the head of one of the largest nurseries in this country. New edition, revised up to date. Invaluable to all fruit-growers. Illustrated. Cloth, 12mo. 2.00

The Propagation of Plants.

By Andrew S. Fuller. Illustrated with numerous engravings. An eminently practical and useful work. Describing the process of hybridizing and crossing species and varieties, and also the many different modes by which cultivated plants may be propagated and multiplied. Cloth, 12mo 1.50

Stewart's Shepherd's Manual.

A Valuable Practical Treatise on the Sheep, for American farmers and sheep growers. It is so plain that a farmer, or a farmer's son, who has never kept a sheep, may learn from its pages how to manage a flock successfully, and yet so complete that even the experienced shepherd may gather many suggestions from it. The results of personal experience of some years with the characters of the various modern breeds of sheep, and the sheep-raising capabilities of many portions of our extensive territory and that of Canada—and the careful study of the diseases to which our sheep are chiefly subject, with those by which they may eventually be afflicted through unforeseen accidents—as well as the methods of management called for under our circumstances, are here gathered. By Henry Stewart. Illustrated. Cloth, 12mo.... 1.50

Allen's American Cattle.

Their History, Breeding, and Management. By Lewis F. Allen. This Book will be considered indispensable by every breeder of live stock. The large experience of the author in improving the character of American herds adds to the weight of his observations, and has enabled him to produce a work which will at once make good his claims as a standard authority on the subject. New and revised edition. Illustrated. Cloth, 12mo 2 50

Fuller's Grape Culturist.

By. A. S. Fuller. This is one of the very best of works on the culture of the hardy grapes, with full directions for all departments of propagation, culture, etc., with 150 excellent engravings, illustrating planting, training, grafting, etc. Cloth, 12mo 1.50

White's Cranberry Culture.

CONTENTS:—Natural History.—History of Cultivation.—Choice of Location.—Preparing the Ground.—Planting the Vines.—Management of Meadows.—Flooding—Enemies and Difficulties Overcome.—Picking.—Keeping.—Profit and Loss.—Letters from Practical Growers.—Insects Injurious to the Cranberry. By Joseph J. White. A practical grower. Illustrated. Cloth, 12mo. New and revised edition. 1.25

Herbert's Hints to Horse-Keepers.

This is one of the best and most popular works on the Horse in this country. A Complete Manual for Horsemen, embracing: How to Breed a Horse; How to Buy a Horse; How to Break a Horse; How to Use a Horse; How to Feed a Horse; How to Physic a Horse (Allopathy or Homœopathy); How to Groom a Horse; How to Drive a Horse; How to Ride a Horse, etc. By the late Henry William Herbert (Frank Forester). Beautifully Illustrated. Cloth, 12mo... 1.75

Henderson's Practical Floriculture.

By Peter Henderson. A guide to the successful propagation and cultivation of florists' plants. The work is not one for florists and gardeners only, but the amateur's wants are constantly kept in mind, and we have a very complete treatise on the cultivation of flowers under glass, or in the open air, suited to those who grow flowers for pleasure as well as those who make them a matter of trade. The work is characterized by the same radical common sense that marked the author's "Gardening for Profit," and it holds a high place in the estimation of lovers of agriculture. Beautifully illustrated. New and enlarged edition. Cloth, 12mo..................................... 1.50

Harris's Talks on Manures.

By Joseph Harris, M. S., author of " Walks and Talks on the Farm," "Harris on the Pig," etc. Revised and enlarged by the author. A series of familiar and practical talks between the author and the deacon, the doctor, and other neighbors, on the whole subject of manures and fertilizers ; including a chapter specially written for it by Sir John Bennet Lawes, of Rothamsted, England. Cloth, 12mo........... 1.75

Waring's Draining for Profit and Draining for Health.

This book is a very complete and practical treatise, the directions in which are plain, and easily followed. The subject of thorough farm drainage is discussed in all its bearings, and also that more extensive land drainage by which the sanitary condition of any district may be greatly improved, even to the banishment of fever and ague, typhoid and malarious fever. By Geo. E. Waring, Jr   Illustrated, Cloth 12mo.
1.50

The Practical Rabbit-Keeper.

By Cuniculus. Illustrated. A comprehensive work on keeping and raising Rabbits for pleasure as well as for profit. The book is abundantly illustrated with all the various Courts, Warrens, Hutches, Fencing, etc., and also with excellent portraits of the most important species of rabbits throughout the world. 12mo.................. 1.50

Quinby's New Bee-Keeping.

The Mysteries of Bee-keeping Explained. Combining the results of Fifty Years' Experience, with the latest discoveries and inventions, and presenting the most approved methods, forming a complete work. Cloth, 12mo 1.50

Profits in Poultry.

Useful and Ornamental Breeds and their Profitable Management. This excellent work contains the combined experience of a number of practical men in all departments of poultry raising. It is profusely illustrated and forms an unique and important addition to our poultry literature. Cloth, 12mo.. 1.00

Barn Plans and Outbuildings.

Two Hundred and Fifty-seven Illustrations. A most Valuable Work, full of Ideas, Hints, Suggestions, Plans, etc., for the Construction of Barns and Outbuildings, by Practical writers. Chapters are devoted, among other subjects, to the Economic Erection and Use of Barns. Grain Barns, House Barns, Cattle Barns, Sheep Barns, Corn Houses, Smoke Houses, Ice Houses, Pig Pens, Granaries, etc. There are likewise chapters upon Bird Houses, Dog Houses, Tool Sheds, Ventilators, Roofs and Roofing, Doors and Fastenings, Work Shops, Poultry Houses, Manure Sheds, Barn Yards, Root Pits, etc. Recently published. Cloth, 12mo........ .... 1.50

Parsons on the Rose.

By Samuel B. Parsons. A treatise on the propagation, culture, and history of the rose. New and revised edition. In his work upon the rose, Mr. Parsons has gathered up the curious legends concerning the flower, and gives us an idea of the esteem in which it was held in former times. A simple garden classification has been adopted, and the leading varieties under each class enumerated and briefly described. The chapters on multiplication, cultivation, and training are very full, and the work is altogether one of the most complete before the public. Illustrated. Cloth, 12mo....................1.00

Heinrich's Window Flower Garden.

The author is a practical florist, and this enterprising volume embodies his personal experiences in Window Gardening during a long period. New and enlarged edition. By Julius J. Heinrich. Fully Illustrated. Cloth, 12mo.. .75

Liautard's Chart of the Age of the Domestic Animals.

Adopted by the United States Army. Enables one to accurately determine the age of horses, cattle, sheep, dogs, and pigs.......... .50

Pedder's Land Measurer for Farmers.

A convenient Pocket Companion, showing at once the contents of any piece of land, when its length and width are known, up to 1,500 feet either way, with various other useful farm tables. Cloth, 18mo; .60

How to Plant and What to Do with the Crops.

With other valuable hints for the Farm, Garden and Orchard. By Mark W. Johnson. Illustrated. CONTENTS : Times for Sowing Seeds :. Covering Seeds ; Field Crops ; Garden or Vegetable Seeds, Sweet Herbs, etc.; Tree Seeds ; Flower Seeds ; Fruit Trees ; Distances Apart for Fruit Trees and Shrubs ; Profitable Farming ; Green or Manuring Crops ; Root Crops ; Forage Plants ; What to do with the Crops ; The Rotation of Crops ; Varieties ; Paper Covers, post-paid.......... .50

Your Plants.

Plain and Practical Directions for the Treatment of Tender and Hardy Plants in the House and in the Garden. By James Sheehan. The above title well describes the character of the work—"Plain and Practical." The author, a commercial florist and gardener, has endeavored, in this work, to answer the many questions asked by his customers, as to the proper treatment of plants. The book shows all through that its author is a practical man, and he writes as one with a large store of experience. The work better meets the wants of the amateur who grows a few plants in the window, or has a small flower Garden, than a larger treatise intended for those who cultivate plants upon a more extended-scale. Price, post-paid, paper covers................... .40

Husmann's American Grape-Growing and Wine-Making.

By George Husmann of Talcoa vineyards, Napa, California. New and enlarged edition. With contributions from well-known grape-growers, giving a wide range of experience. The author of this book is a recognized authority on the subject. Cloth, 12mo................ 1.50

The Scientific Angler.

A general and instructive work on Artistic Angling, by the late David Foster. Complied by his Sons. With an Introductory Chapter and Copious Foot Notes, by William C. Harris, Editor of the "American Angler." Cloth, 12mo.................................... 1.50

Keeping One Cow.
A collection of Prize Essays, and selections from a number of other Essays, with editorial notes, suggestions, etc. This book gives the latest information, and in a clear and condensed form, upon the management of a single Milch Cow. Illustrated with full-page engravings of the most famous dairy cows. Recently published. Cloth, 12mo 1.00

Law's Veterinary Adviser
A Guide to the Prevention and Treatment of Disease in Domestic Animals. This is one of the best works on this subject, and is especially designed to supply the need of the busy American Farmer, who can rarely avail himself of the advice of a Scientific Veterinarian. It is brought up to date and treats of the Prevention of Disease, as well as of the Remedies. By Prof. Jas. Law. Cloth, Crown 8vo...... 3.00

Guenon's Treatise on Milch Cows.
A Treatise on the Bovine Species in General. An entirely new translation of the last edition of this popular and instructive book. By Thos. J. Hand, Secretary of the American Jersey Cattle Club. With over 100 Illustrations, especially engraved for this work. Cloth, 12mo.
1.00

The Cider Maker's Handbook.
A complete guide for making and keeping pure cider. By J. M. Trowbridge. Fully Illustrated. Cloth, 12mo........................... 1.00

Long's Ornamental Gardening for Americans.
A treatise on Beautifying Homes, Rural Districts, and Cemeteries. A plain and practical work at a moderate price, with numerous illustrations, and instructions so plain that they may be readily followed. By Elias A. Long. Landscape Architect. Illustrated. Cloth, 12mo.
2.00

The Dogs of Great Britain, America and Other Countries.
New, enlarged and revised edition. Their breeding, training and management, in health and disease ; comprising all the essential parts of the two standard works on the dog, by "Stonehenge," thereby furnishing for $2 what once cost $11.25. Contains Lists of all Premiums given at the last Dog Shows. It Describes the Best Game and Hunting Grounds in America. Contains over One Hundred Beautiful Engravings, embracing most noted Dogs in both Continents, making together, with Chapters by American Writers, the most Complete Dog Book ever published. Cloth, 12mo.......................... 2.00

Stewart's Feeding Animals.
By Elliot W. Stewart. A new and valuable practical work upon the laws of animal growth, specially applied to the rearing and feeding horses, cattle, diary cows, sheep and swine. Illustrated. Cloth, 12mo.
2.00

How to Co-operate.
A Manual for Co-operators. By Herbert Myrick. This book describes the how rather than the wherefore of co-operation. In other words it tells how to manage a co-operative store, farm or factory, and co-operative dairying, banking and fire insurance, and co-operative farmers' and women's exchanges for both buying and selling. The directions given are based on the actual experience of successful co-operative enterprises in all parts of the United States. The character and usefulness of the book commend it to the attention of all men and women who desire to better their condition. 12mo. Cloth.............. 1.50

Batty's Practical Taxidermy and Home Decoration.

By Joseph H. Batty, taxidermist for the government surveys and many colleges and museums in the United States. An entirely new and complete as well as authentic work on taxidermy—giving in detail full directions for collecting and mounting animals, birds, reptiles, fish, insects, and general objects of natural history. 125 illustrations. Cloth, 12mo. 1.50

Stewart's Irrigation for the Farm, Garden, and Orchard.

New and Enlarged Edition. This work is offered to those American Farmers, and other cultivators of the soil, who from painful experience can readily appreciate the losses which result from the scarcity of water at critical periods. By Henry Stewart. Fully illustrated. Cloth, 12mo 1.50

Johnson's How Crops Grow.

New Edition, entirely rewritten. A Treatise on the Chemical Composition, Structure, and Life of the Plant. Revised Edition. This book is a guide to the knowledge of agricultural plants, their composition, their structure, and modes of development and growth ; of the complex organization of plants, and the use of the parts ; the germination of seeds, and the food of plants obtained both from the air and the soil. The book is an invaluable one to all real students of agriculture. With numerous illustrations and tables of analysis. By Prof. Samuel W. Johnson, of Yale College. Cloth, 12mo 2.00

Johnson's How Crops Feed.

A treatise on the Atmosphere and the Soil, as related in the Nutrition of Agricultural Plants. The volume—the companion and complement to "How Crops Grow,"—has been welcomed by those who appreciate scientific aspects of agriculture. Illustrated. By Prof. Samuel W. Johnson. Cloth, 12mo 2.00

Warington's Chemistry of the Farm.

Treating with the utmost clearness and conciseness, and in the most popular manner possible, of the relations of Chemistry to Agriculture, and providing a welcome manual for those, who, while not having time to systematically study Chemistry, will gladly have such an idea as this gives them of its relation to operations on the farm. By R. Warington, F. C. S. Cloth, 12mo 1.00

French's Farm Drainage.

The Principles, Process, and Effects of Draining Land, with Stones, Wood, Ditch-plows, Open Ditches, and especially with Ties ; including Tables of Rainfall, Evaporation, Filteration, Excavation, Capacity of Pipes, cost and number to the acre. By Judge French, of New Hampshire. Cloth, 12mo 1.50

Hunter and Trapper.

The best modes of Hunting and Trapping are fully explained, and Foxes, Deer, Bears, etc., fall into his traps readily by following his directions. By Halsey Thrasher, an old and experienced sportsman. Cloth, 12mo .... .75

The American Merino. For Wool or for Mutton.

A practical and most valuable work on the selection, care, breeding and diseases of the Merino sheep, in all sections of the the the United States. It is a full and exhaustive treatise upon this one breed of sheep, By Stephen Powers. Cloth, 12mo .... 1..

Armatage's Every Man His Own Horse Doctor.

By Prof. George Armatage, M. R. C. V. S. A valuable and comprehensive guide for both the professional and general reader with the fullest and latest information regarding all diseases, local injuries, lameness, operations, poisons, the dispensatory, etc , etc., with practical anatomical and surgical Illustrations. New Edition. Together with Blaine's "Veterinary Art," and numerous recipes. One large 8vo. volume, 830 pages, half morocco............................ 7.50

Dadd's Modern Horse Doctor.

Containing Practical Observations on the Causes, Nature, and Treatment of Diseases and Lameness of Horses—embracing recent and improved Methods, according to an enlightened system of Veterinary Practice, for Preservation and Restoration of Health. Illustrated. By Geo. H. Dadd, M. D. V. S., Cloth, 12mo...................... 1.50

The Family Horse.

Its Stabling, Care, and Feeding. By Geo. A. Martin. A Practical Manual, full of the most useful information. Illustrated. Cloth, 12mo 1.00

Sander's Horse Breeding.

Being the general principles of Heredity applied to the Business of Breeding Horses and the Management of Stallions, Brood Mares and Foals. The book embraces all that the breeder should know in regard to the selection of stock, management of the stallion, brood mare, and foal, and treatment of diseases peculiar to breeding animals. By J. H. Sanders. 12mo, cloth..................................... 2.00

Coburn's Swine Husbandry.

New, revised and enlarged edition. The Breeding, Rearing and Management of Swine, and the Prevention and Treatment of their Diseases. It is the fullest and freshest compendium relating to Swine Breeding yet offered. By F. D. Coburn. Cloth, 12mo......... 1.75

Dadd's American Cattle Doctor.

By George H. Dadd, M. D., Veterinary Practitioner. To help every man to be his own cattle-doctor; giving the necessary information for preserving the health and curing the diseases of oxen, cows, sheep, and swine, with a great variety of original recipes, and valuable information on farm and dairy management. Cloth, 12mo............ 1.50

Silos, Ensilage, and Silage.

A practical treatise on the Ensilage of Fodder Corn. Containing the most recent and authentic information on this important subject, by Manly Miles, M.D., F.R.M.S. Illustrated. Cloth 12mo......... .50

Broom Corn and Brooms.

A Treatise on Raising Broom-Corn and Making Brooms on a small or Large Scale. Illustrated. 12mo. Cloth cover.................... .50

American Bird Fancier.

Or how to breed, rear, and care for Song and Domestic Birds. This valuable and important little work for all who are interested in the keeping of Song Birds, has been revised and enlarged, and is now a complete manual upon the subject. All who own valuable birds, or wish to do so, will find the new Fancier indispensable. New, revised and enlarged edition. By D. J. Browne, and Dr. Fuller Walker. Illustrated, paper cover... .50

Armatage's Every Man His Own Cattle Doctor.

The Veterinary Cyclopedia—Embracing all the practical information of value heretofore published on the Diseases of Cattle, Sheep, and Swine, together with the latest and best information regarding all known diseases up to the present time. Compiled and edited by that eminent authority, Prof. George Armatage, M. R. C. V. S. One large octavo volume, 894 pages, with upwards of 350 practical illustrations, showing forms of disease and treatment. Half morocco. 7.50

Onions—How to Raise them Profitably.

Being the Practical Details, from Selection of Seed and Preparation of Ground to Harvesting and Marketing the Crop, given very plainly by Seventeen Practical Onion Growers of long experience residing in different parts of the country. No more valuable work of its size was ever issued. Paper cover, 8vo............................ .20

Tobacco Culture—Full Practical Details.

This useful and valuable work contains full details of every process from the Selection and Preparation of the Seed and Soil to the Harvesting, Curing and Marketing the Crop, with illustrative engravings of the operations. The work was prepared by Fourteen Experienced Tobacco Growers, residing in different parts of the country. It also contains notes on the Tobacco Worm, with illustrations, 8vo,.. .25

Hop Culture.

Plain directions given by ten experienced cultivators. Revised, enlarged and edited by A. S. Fuller. Forty engravings............ .30

Flax Culture.

A very valuable work, containing full directions, from selection of ground and seed to preparation and marketing of crop, as given by a number of experienced growers, 8vo........................... .30

Potato Pests.

No Farmer can afford to be without this little book. It gives the most complete account of the Colorado Beetle anywhere to be found, and includes all the latest discoveries as to the habits of the insect and the various means for its destruction. It is well illustrated, and exhibits in a map the spread of the insect since it left its native home. By Prof. C. V. Riley. Paper cover...... .... .50

Home Fishing and Home Waters.

By Seth Green. The Utilization of Farm Streams; Management of Fish in the Artificial Pond; Transportation of Eggs and Fry, etc. Cloth, 12mo.. .50

Reed's House Plans for Everybody.

By S. B. Reed. This useful volume meets the wants of persons of moderate means, and gives a wide range of design, from a dwelling costing $250 up to $8,000, and adapted to farm, village and town residences. Nearly all of these plans have been tested by practical workings. One feature of the work imparts a value over any similar publication of the kind that we have seen. It gives an estimate of the quantity of every article used in the construction, and the cost of each article at the time the building was erected or the design made. Even if prices vary from time to time, one can, from these data, ascertain within a few dollars the probable cost of constructing any one of the buildings here presented. Profusely illustrated. Cloth, black and gold, 12mo.. 1.50

Gregory on Cabbages—How to Grow Them.

A Practical Treatise on Cabbage Culture, giving full details on every point, including Keeping and Marketing the Crop. By James J. H. Gregory. Paper cover, 12mo............................. .30

Gregory on Carrots, Mangold-Wurtzels, etc.

How to raise them, how to keep them, and how to feed them. By J. J. H. Gregory. Paper Cover, 12mo........................... .30

Gregory on Onion Raising.

What kinds to raise, and the way to raise them. By J. J. H. Gregory. Paper cover, 12mo.. .30

Gregory on Squashes.

This Treatise, which no Farmer or Gardener ought to be without, tells all about selecting the soil for squashes; how much Manure is necessary; how to prepare and Plant; about Hoeing and Cultivating; Setting of the Fruit; Ripening, Gathering, Storing, Care during Winter, etc. By J. J. H. Gregory. Paper cover, 12mo............... .30

Hog-Raising and Pork-Making.

By Rufus Bacon Martin. The hog is reared for the money that is in him, and he represents either a profit or loss to his owner according to the treatment he receives. This pamphlet gives the personal research and experience of the author, contains many valuable suggestions, and answers many of the questions that arise in the business of hog-raising. Paper, 12mo.. .40

Fulton's Peach Culture.

This is the only practical guide to Peach Culture on the Delaware Peninsula, and is the best work upon the subject of peach growing for those who would be successful in that culture in any part of the country. It has been thoroughly revised and a large portion of it re-written, by Hon. J. Alexander Fulton, the author, bringing it down to date. Cloth, 12mo.... .... 1.50

Silk Culture.

A Handbook for Silk-Growers. By Mrs. C. E. Bamford. CONTENTS.—Chapter I. The Mulberry.—II. Gathering the Leaves.—III. The Cocoonery.—IV. Eggs of the Silk Worm Moth.—V. Feeding the Silk Worms.—VI. Moulting.—VII. Spinning.—VIII. The Cocoons.—IX. The Moths of the Silk Worm.—X. Varieties of Silk Worms.—XI. Diseases of the Silk Worm.—XII. Reeling.—XIII. Chemistry of Silk.—XIV. Miscellaneous. Paper, 12mo. Price, postpaid. -- .30

Treats' Injurious Insects of the Farm and Garden. By Mrs. Mary Treat.

An original investigator who has added much to our knowledge of both Plants and insects, and those who are familiar with Darwin's works are aware that he gives her credit for important observation and discoveries. New and Enlarged Edition. With an Illustrated Chapter on Beneficial Insects. Fully illustrated. Cloth, 12mo.......... 2.00

Fuller's Small Fruit Culturist.

By Andrew S. Fuller. Rewritten, enlarged, and brought fully up to the present time. The book covers the whole ground of propagating small fruits, their culture, varieties, packing for market, etc. It is very finely and thoroughly illustrated, and makes an admirable companion to "The Grape Culturist," by the same well known author.
1.50

www.ingramcontent.com/pod-product-compliance
Lightning Source LLC
Chambersburg PA
CBHW032007010726
47493CB00007B/2308